CHALFORD
Oral History
S E R I E S

DEVIZES
voices

Olive Chivers' Grandpa Willis and family. Olive, whose mother is Ethel, the little girl on the right, describes her childhood at the family house in St Johns Street in the 1920s.

CHALFORD
Oral History
SERIES

DEVIZES
voices

Compiled by
David Buxton

CHALFORD

First published 1996
Copyright © David Buxton, 1996

The Chalford Publishing Company
St Mary's Mill, Chalford,
Stroud, Gloucestershire, GL6 8NX

ISBN 0 7524 0661 2

Typesetting and origination by
The Chalford Publishing Company
Printed in Great Britain by
Redwood Books, Trowbridge

Devizes' ladies' football team in about 1948 . They were, back row, left to right: Mabel Buckland (trainer), Mary Lloyd, Jacky Townsend, Phyllis Lovelock, Mary Wheeler, Mary Fowler, Flossie Laver (trainer). Front row: Josette Townsend, Doreen Underwood, Fiona Townsend, Pat Rowles, Sybil Kirby, Joan Giddings.

CONTENTS

Miss Maud Bowsher, who ran the ironmongers shop with her two sisters in the Market Place, dressed as Katisha for the 1923 production of *The Mikado* in the Corn Exchange.

INTRODUCTION

The text of this book is made up entirely of the memories of Devizes people, gathered with a few exceptions, over a period of about eighteen months using a tape recorder in informal interviews. They were made mostly by the fireside in the comfort of the interviewees' homes.

It has always been a fascination to me to listen to older people's memories. I remember listening to my grandmother telling me, a long time ago, about her childhood and finding that it was often the small details about days gone by that were the most interesting. She once remarked that the streets *smelled* different in her childhood. Because horses were used everywhere for transport there was a smell of horses in the streets. Because trams were the common form of public transport in Derby where she

The junction of Sidmouth and Estcourt Streets photographed by John Chivers in about 1900.

grew up there was also a smell of 'ozone' in the air, created probably by sparking of the electric cables that the trams ran on. I remember thinking at the time that, 'you wouldn't find that in a history book!' There are many things like that, which are not recorded in books because they are not things of political or economic importance, but if you really want to know what it was like to live at a time before your own, you need to listen to ordinary people's memories, or what is more usually called nowadays, 'oral history'. Fortunately, it is now generally agreed that the recording of people's memories of events, work experi-

ences, school and so on, is to be viewed as a serious activity which is just as important as the more traditional methods of recording and archiving the past. Many public record offices and libraries now have a 'sound archive' which collects taped reminiscences of local people and amateur local history groups are springing up all over the country with the express purpose of collecting taped interviews. There is even a national Oral History Society whose aim is to promote the recording of 'people's histories', to advise on ways of doing it and on the utilisation of the material produced.

Oral history is not the precise 'science' that many other historical methods may claim to be. Inevitably, memory plays tricks on us and we don't always recall exactly what happened even though we feel sure we've got it right. Compare your memory of an event in childhood with that of someone else's recollection of it, there will probably be a few discrepancies. Some 'memories' grow and change with the telling. Every family has some favourite stories that are brought out occasionally and retold, so much that some members feel that they actually remember them, even though they were not there at the time or were too small to have a real memory of it! While such tales probably have the core of real truth in them, it is always difficult to know how much has been added later. More reliable, and often more interesting, are the memories that people recall for the first time in many years, perhaps hardly recalled since the events described actually took place. It was a common experience for me, while collecting the memories in this book, for someone to say, when approached about an interview, I'm afraid I won't be much use, I can't remember a lot', but only minutes into a conversation memories, stimulated by questions about childhood, would usually come flooding back. Often these recollections appeared as fresh ones, recalling people and places not thought about for many years.

Apart from the important matter of saving oral history for posterity there is another good reason for collecting people's memories - most of us find reminiscences quite irresistible and fascinating! Without exception, I think, people I interviewed for this book enjoyed the opportunity of recalling their earlier days when asked to do so. There is pleasure to be had for the teller and the listener in oral history! Most of us indulge in a lot of reminiscing when we meet with old friends, it's a pleasant and reassuring activity, and the older you are the more memories you have to recall! When older people feel 'stranded' in the modern world, talking about the old days can often restore confidence and even mental health. Care workers now use reminiscence sessions formally, to help groups of old people to relate again to each other and to their surroundings, through the common ground of the 'old days'.

Most of the people whose memories are included in this book are living in Devizes today but I have included extracts from two interviews that were made some time ago: one of these was with Lillian Hinxman who was born in High Street in 1895 and died in Salisbury in 1995. I met her at her home in Salisbury in 1985 and recorded her memories of life in Devizes at the turn of the century. The second of these earlier interviews was with Maudie Dunford who related stories of her childhood to me at her home in The Island, Devizes in 1983.

The reminiscences brought together here cover quite a wide range of experience of life in Devizes in the first half of the century, ranging from those of the fairly comfortably off, with maids to do the cooking and cleaning, to those who survived with the help of free soup and milk. There is at least one person living in Devizes today who can recall the opening of the Palace cinema in 1912 (and relate events from the first film!) and there are people who can talk about soldiers massing in Devizes during the First World War and the effect this had on the town. There were many family-owned shops in Devizes in pre-war days and the loss of these was an important factor in the altered social and commercial scene in the town. It is therefore interesting to read several first-hand accounts here of 'life over the shop' in those days.

The book is illustrated with old photographs of Devizes which I hope will help to bring alive the accounts that they accompany. Most of these come from the the albums of the people doing the talking but others are from a collection of pictures I have accumulated myself over the years. When transcribing the reminiscences from the tape recordings I have, as far as possible, presented them as they were spoken. A minimum of editing has been done, to improve the readability, but the aim at all times has been to preserve, as far as possible, the spoken word. I hope you will enjoy the experience of reminiscing with these Devizes' people and that in so doing you will recall and enjoy many more memories of your own.

ACKNOWLEDGEMENTS

I would like to thank all those people who have shared their memories with me and by so doing provided the material for this book. I have been warmly entertained by everyone I approached for an interview and collecting the material has been a very enjoyable experience for me. Thank you for your time, your indulgence and all the cups of tea!

Many people loaned photographs which are included here and I thank them for allowing me to use these too. I would like to thank the staff of Devizes Library and the Devizes Museum library for their help.

David Buxton
Devizes
October 1996

Children playing in Jeffrey's Court, Sheep Street in the early 1930s. Mrs Pithouse stands in front of the house that belonged to the Underwoods. The arch behind her leads out to the street. The door on the right is the shared wash-house. The little boy at the front is Geoff Underwood.

Gladys Hiscock entertains a group of children in Jeffrey's Court, Sheep Street in about 1934. The children are Joan Strudely, Don Hyde, Doreen Underwood and Ralph Merrett.

Outgrowing the House

I was born in Sheep Street and was one of ten children. Our house was not very big, we had the shop in the front, a very small room at the back, a cellar and three rooms upstairs. As the family grew we moved the gas stove down into the cellar and did the cooking down there. As we grew, the older ones would go off and live with other members of the family. My sister lived with my grandmother in 25, Long Street and a brother lived with my aunt Bess in Sheep Street, who had a sweet shop, and so on.

In the yard we had one wash-house shared between the families, an outside tap, and one outside toilet for three houses. One morning I looked out of my window and all I could see of our neighbour's toilet was the roof, it had sunk completely into a hole! Luckily no-one was in it at the time.

Bill Underwood

Swings on the Green

We didn't have a big garden behind the shop but we used to play in the studio when it wasn't being used for taking photographs. I used to go to the Green to play with my older sister. She was eight years older than me. One day I got concussed! We were playing on the swings, I was sitting down and she was standing up, working the swing, when some other children came up and want-

12

ed us to get off. I remember saying, 'No, go on Doris, go higher!', but that was the last I remembered because someone grabbed hold of the iron stay of the swing and we went flying! My sister, because she was higher up, fell onto the grass but I fell head first onto the concrete and knocked myself out. I was wearing a big straw hat and perhaps that saved me from a worse injury. I came round, bit by bit, and I recall my sister asking me if I wanted to go home. I sat for a while in our backyard then the doctor came and I had to sit in a darkened room for some time. The doctor said we should sue the family but of course we didn't do that, in fact, I think my mother ending up helping them, they were a poor family and she gave them some of my old clothes. I don't think we were allowed on the swings again!

Barbara Wickett

Pocket Money

I used to have a comic on Saturday mornings called *Playbox* which cost tuppence and I bought it from Mr Hitchin's shop on the corner of Sheep Street. You could buy some comics for a penny which were printed all in one colour, usually pink or blue, *Comic Cuts* was one of these. My family was friendly with the Hitchins. Percy Hitchins came from Weymouth and stayed in Devizes after the First World War to run the shop which later became Ducks.

One of my favourite sweets was Melford Violets, they were thruppence a packet and were all done up in silver paper - I didn't buy them very often because that was a lot for sweets. Most kids didn't have more than about a ha'penny to spend at a time on sweets. I suppose I was lucky because my grandmother, who lived with us, used to give me a penny every dinner-time as I went back to school. I used to go up to Miss Mead's shop in Sheep Street, near where the library is now, she had a little sweet shop on the corner. My husband's auntie also had a shop in Sheep Street which sold sweets and she used to sell cold rice pudding cut into pieces and sold for a penny a piece! There were about four sweet shops in Sheep Street when I was little.

Joyce Rose

Soup Kitchens

In about 1930 you could get free soup at a place behind the Shambles. We used to queue up with a big jug and get it filled up with soup. It was quite nice too! They were a charity of some sort that gave it out every day. There were seven of us in our family, we slept three to a bed. We lived in Sowerby's Yard in Sheep Street. We'd also go and see 'Nobby' Clark at the church in Long Street, everyday, and get a pint of milk free. They were hard days then, real hard days.

Charlie Stevens

Saturday Mission

On Saturday mornings Miss Cunnington ran a mission class where all the children of High Street

The Fell family of Dyehouse Lane in about 1920. They are, from left to right: Cath, Ethel, Harry, Frank, Bill, Jack (front), Rosie, Ivy, Dolly, Marje.

used to go at about ten o'clock. At the age of about six years my friend Tom and I went along although we were not much interested in making things for the missionaries. What fascinated us was Miss Cunnington's teeth. When she talked her teeth would move up and down in her mouth! She wore an old bonnet with violets on the top.

Violet Scudamore

Walks to Nursteed

We were born in what was then called York Terrace which is now part of Brickley Lane. There is a terrace of town houses on each side of where Bricksteed Avenue now comes out, although that wasn't there in those days. There were allotments on each side and a little track that led through to Nursteed Road. I thought I lived in the country then. There was a hayfield opposite our house and among my earliest memories is the smell of hay and also

The choir of St Mary's church in the 1930s.

of elderberries. That was the end of the town, there was nothing beyond us except Jump Farm. It was a nice walk for us to go down to Nursteed village; the first excitement would be to see the pig sties which were on the left-hand side behind black palings. We had to be lifted up to see over them when we were small but as we got older we could see for ourselves by standing on tiptoes. Then there were ducks on the pond just beyond there and then when you got out onto the Nursteed Road there was the Chivers' saw-mills to look at. They had a great big gantry with a crane on it and we liked to watch that moving up and down.

Olive Chivers

Pocket Money

If ever we had a penny we would go to Little Strongs for some sweets or we would go half way up The Brittox to Willis's the toy shop. It was dark shop and as you went to the back there was a table with penny objects on it - we would spend half an hour looking at them all and then choose one. That was wonderful.

Lillian Hinxman

15

The children of Joseph Strong photographed by John Chivers in 1914. They are, from left to right: Verna, Phyllis, baby Phillip, Leonard and Stewart.

Gales

There was a terrible gale one night which blew down lots of the trees in Quakers Walk. I think it must have been about 1928 or '29. We went for a walk to see them the day after. I think it was the same night that the Unicorn pub across the road from our house had a chimney fire with sparks blowing everywhere. I was at home but my mother and sister were at St Mary's Church and during the service one of the pinnacles was blown off.

Barbara Wickett

Summers on Roundway Down

In my childhood tuberculosis, or consumption, was a killer and it seemed to affect some families badly and could often result in the deaths of several members of a household. There was no cure for it and the only treatment was fresh air. We had some cousins who were older than us, they were adults when we were still children, and consumption attacked them. There were four of them, Mildred, Daisy, Ethel and George and all but Daisy had consumption and died within a short time of each other. They were all adult and married by this time. Mildred married Harry Taplin who had a fish shop in

The Brittox, just up from Pritchard's the men's outfitters. The Taplins also had a small tobacconists and newsagents shop in The Brittox where my cousin Mildred worked. She was not well and my mother used to go into the shop and help her but she died. Doctors recommended people with consumption should sleep in tents or with the windows open. I knew someone who lived in Hartmoor who had consumption and had to sleep in a bell-tent right through a cold winter!

When they were young my brother and sister had swollen tuberculer glands in the neck and they both had operations to treat them. When we were young we enjoyed cutting out things from books and once I was in our nursery at home with my brother and sister when we decided to get down one of my

mother's fashion picture books that she kept for us and in climbing onto the table to reach the shelf I scratched my leg on a pair of scissors held by my brother. It was only a superficial wound but later the wound began to gather and became infected. It was later decided that it had become a tuberculer sore and it went from bad to worse. The doctor, Mr G.S.A.Waylen, [father of Dr George Waylen] was a very reputable person although not, I believe, a trained doctor, came to see me one Sunday afternoon and cut a hole in my leg. He plugged the wound with a long piece of gauze to drain it which was replaced every day. I was only four years old at the time but I can remember the dreadful ordeal of this treatment. Later I went to Devizes Hospital and had the leg operated on, the doctor 'scraped the bone', after

Summer on Roundway Hill in 1914. The portable wooden hut was built for the Strong family by W.E. Chivers. Stewart, is on the left, baby Verna is on Miss Hatton's lap, Mrs Strong stands in the doorway, Leonard stands by his sister, Phyllis, and their aunt sits in a deck chair.

Miss Hatton fries bacon for breakfast at one of the Strong family's summer camps on Roundway Hill in about 1914.

the dew pond used to be. My mother took the bedsteads, the harmonium for hymns on Sunday, a primus stove and a little oven. We even took the canary! We had a bell tent and hired a shepherd's hut, as well, which we children slept in. The main door latched from the outside and was in two halves, like a stable door. When we went to bed we closed the door from the outside and then crawled in through the dog hole where the sheep dog would have got in!

Father used to buy some pullets in the market and they would scratch about around the bungalow, and lay eggs, and we would gradually eat them whilst we were there. We walked down to Heddington and got milk from a farm and bread and provisions from the village. Drinking water was stored in a milk churn hired from the dairy which was filled up for us twice a week by a nearby farmer.

Each morning we went down to the dew pond to wash. The pond was surrounded by railings to stop the cattle from churning up the edge of it but it didn't stop the sheep from getting through to it to drink. We used to climb on the fence and balance on the rails. It was an idyllic time for us, we just ran around and had a wonderful time. Those times are the ones I would most like to relive if I could choose a time to have again.

On Sundays we walked down to Heddington Church, listening to the bells ringing down below us as we walked. We would leave our camp all open with no fear of anyone molesting it. Sometimes, people came to stay with us, my uncle from Bristol once stayed and Aunt Louie and Uncle Ebenezer, who had the jewellers shop in the

which I could not walk for a while and to my utter shame was pushed about in a pram! Eventually it cleared up but I still have the scar.

My parents decided that as we all appeared to have tuberculer susceptibility they should try to do something about it. As fresh air was considered to be the only treatment, my father had a sectional, wooden bungalow built by W.E. Chivers so that we could all go up onto Roundway Hill and spend time there in the fresh air. Each summer from 1910 to the beginning of the First World War the whole family lived for a month or so up there. The spot was not far from the top of the hill near where

A childrens' Christmas party at the British Legion hall in Station Road in *c.* 1955.

Market Place, also came once came to stay. That one did not work out very well and they were not asked to come again. My mother didn't agree with Uncle Eb', especially when he once went into the market and bought cheap over-ripe bananas which didn't last well in the bungalow!

During The War my father sold the bungalow to his brother, Uncle Eb, who took it to Codford, where the Australian Expeditionary Force were camped, and opened it as a little shop. My brother was allowed to go and stay with him for a while but I was thought to be too young at the time.

After the war my brother and I, both by this time at Dauntsey's School having won scholarships, felt we would like to camp again on the hill but we no longer had the bungalow. We hired a

marquee from Chivers and camped there several times over the next few years. It was just as good!

Leonard Strong

Clothes

My mother bought my first ready-made coat from Lucas's in the Market Place. All my coats and clothes before that had been made by Miss Gray who lived round by the Green. The first coat I had after I started at the Secondary School was made by her, it cost 25/- and it was a brown herring-bone tweed. There were lots of dress-makers in town. Another one we used to go to was upstairs in Handel House, the door to it was up in the corner

19

The 'small' charabanc ready for a pleasure trip. Butcher Bert Sanders sits near the front with his wife, Blanche (standing), and son, Tom, c. 1923.

round on the lefthand side, run by Miss Best and her sister.

Joyce Rose

A Young Poacher

As a child I wanted passionately to breed foreign moths but to do this you needed money to buy the eggs first. Not large amounts really, shillings usually, but out of the reach of most small boys in the 1930s, if you got sixpence a week you were lucky. I had seen an advert in the *Boys Own Paper*, given to me by a friend, for 'Giant Moths of the Jungle' and I sent for a catalogue and instructions on breeding them for which I managed to scrape together the sixpence needed. When I got this I was able to see the prices I would have to find to get some, but how was I to find the money? Living next to the fields I was aware that the country was swarming with rabbits and in my wanderings about the fields I often encountered casual poachers who took no notice of a small boy watching them. It was here that I learnt the art of snaring, not illegal then, but the poaching was! A rabbit made a good meal for a family and I was able to get between fourpence and sixpence for one. You left the skin on it because the person who bought it would expect to get a penny for that from someone else! Getting rid of them was a bit difficult for me but my grandmother was helpful - she managed to sell a few to the neighbours. In this way I got enough money to get started in moth breeding, a hobby that lasted most of my life.

Arthur Cleverly

The tunnel under the castle walls viewed from the wooden footbridge. This is probably a wartime photograph as every bit of spare land is under cultivation.

Sunday School Outings

All the Sunday schools from the churches in Devizes in the old days used to join together for an outing. A train would be chartered from Devizes station to Weymouth. There would be great excitement as all the families came down to the station to see their children off and then back again later to meet them as they came home. The trains had corridors that ran the length of the train and we would walk up and down to find friends who were with other churches. I went with the Methodists. When we got to Weymouth we went our own ways and met up again at the end of the day under the clock.

The churches catered very well for the children in those days. On other occasions there were Sunday School treats at Roundway Park. All the children from different churches marched in procession along the streets to a field just inside the gates to the Park where they each had their allotted space. There would be games and scrambling for sweets. I don't remember anyone suffering from eating these unwrapped sweets after they had been thrown onto the ground although nowadays, I suppose, that would not do! There were summer fetes in Roundway Park and in the castle grounds too.

Miss Kemp

Advertisement for H. & G. Chivers in 1931.

The Yield Book

My father's sister married Mr Sawyer who had the leather goods shop at the top of The Brittox and they lived at Monticello on Potterne Hill. They were very strict chapel and next to the house, which is high up on the hill, they kept a big wooden hoarding on which were displayed texts, to be seen from the road. At home they kept a 'yield book'. Whenever there was a domestic dispute they would consult this book to see who it was that had yielded last time!

Leonard Strong

The Wooden Bridge

The bridge over the railway at the far end of St John's churchyard was always a favourite place for children to play. We could watch the trains go underneath, get a good view of the castle and of the open countryside and if we shouted loudly there was a good echo back from the castle wall.

Tom Sanders

Christmas Fat Stock Show

On one of the last Thursdays before Christmas one of the things I remember going to see was the annual fat stock show in the Shambles. The entrance was closed off and there was an entrance charge to see a display of livestock. Animals were tethered to rails along the walls and at the end up the steps was a big exhibition of moulded butter. It was an exciting event for us, we could hear the cattle from our house in The Brittox. The farmers built a big evergreen arbour around the entrance and out over the pavement which you had to walk through to get into the Shambles. At the Christmas markets the meat for sale was hung all around the entrance. Butchers shops usually had their own slaughterhouses and it was a common sight to see cattle in the streets being driven to market from the railway station or taken back from the market by a farmer or a butcher.

Leonard Strong

Enid (left) and Olive Chivers playing in the garden of 30, St Johns Street behind the family home and shop, c. 1928. The photograph was taken by Mr Reynolds who was a teacher from the Senior School.

The House in St Johns Street

When I was five, in 1923, we moved to St Johns Street which was a shop, a painters and decorators shop, owned by my grandfather. He retired and we moved into his house and he moved into ours. We lived there until after the war. It was called H. & G. Chivers and the firm was three generations in the family. It was a lovely big house, where Leybourne's is now, and it was a good house to grow up in. We loved it as children, it had lots of rooms, although none of them was a really decent size, but it was an interesting house. There were two lots of stairs going up to the first floor and two lots going to the attic and another flight to the cellar. The front attics didn't connect up with the back attics, so you had to go down one flight along a passage and back up another to get there! My

mother didn't like having to move there because really it was quite a headache to cope with. She had loved her first house which was new when she'd got married and moved into it and which she had watched being built from Southbroom School where she taught. There were two sons to look after the family business and when grandfather retired one of them had to move into the house. I don't think my father minded because he grew up there. There were three children in my father's family and only one in his brother's so it made sense for us to move in.

The house went back a long way; on the ground floor was the shop with an office behind it and then behind that was a sitting room. This led into a large hall that was as big as a room, and beyond that was a very nice dining room. From this you had to go up a little passage round the side, which wasn't

Giles Chivers, grandfather of Olive Chivers, and founder of the family plumbing, painting and decorating firm in St Johns Street.

little slope down to the main garden, a large part of which, was given over to fruit stuff which much later I found out was there because father's grandmother had a fruiterer's shop in The Brittox and she must have grown a lot of her fruit here. There were black currants, white currants and red currants, an enormous amount of raspberries, plums and apples and goodness knows what. We made huge quantities of jam. I've still got a letter written by my grandmother, who I didn't know as she died quite young, giving directions about what was to be done about the fruit. She said that Annie the maid (they were all called Annie, whatever their names!) would

Mr Underwood, the hairdresser, with sons, Geoff and Bill (in the cart) in the garden behind Jeffrey's Court in about 1930.

very convenient, to get to the kitchen and then a scullery. Beyond that was a huge garden which went right down to the castle grounds. There were lots of interesting places to play outside too. There was a cobbled courtyard, which is still there, but the cobbles have gone, with access from the street through a passage and an arch between the shops. From this you could go under the house through a big workshop and a glazing shed. Between this and the outside wall was a narrow way where the ladders were kept which, as children, we named 'Ladder Street' which led into an area that was called the drying ground, which was the 'Market Place' to us. All the washing was dried here from our wash-house next to it. Then there was a know how to do this, that and the other.

The painting business lasted just about one hundred years. My brother finally sold it in about 1980. As well as doing the painting and decorating we sold paint, wallpaper and a few other items, like gas mantles, for example.

Olive Chivers

Royal Visit

When Edward VIII was Prince of Wales it became known that he was going to pass through the town and we were all given flags and we practiced waving them at school! When the day came we waited by the railings, for what semed like hours, and then this black car came along, went past and it was all finished! I couldn't understand what all the preparation had been for.

Bill Underwood

Wales to Devizes

My mother was English and my father was a Welsh miner and I was born in Swansea. When my father died in the thirties my mother couldn't make ends meet so we came to Devizes to be with her family. My grandfather had been a coachman for a vicar in Old Park and when the vicar died he became one of the coachman at the Bear Hotel. They had horse-drawn, and later motor buses for hire. My grandmother lived in Sheep Street near to the Town School. It was much easier to live here with small children than in

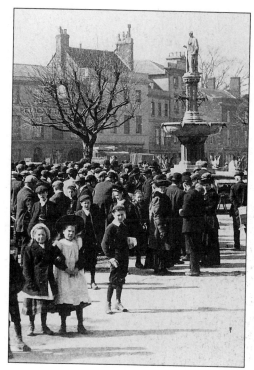

Children in the Market Place, *c*. 1900.

Wales at the time. Whenever my mother had gone for a job there they hadn't given it to her if they heard that she had small children. We had an old aunt who lived in Wedhampton who found us a cottage close to her which was half a crown a week and so we moved. My mother used to go out to confinements and so earned enough to make ends meet. I don't think that my mother ever got used to it here but I loved living in the countryside. From Wedhampton we went to Urchfont where we had a cottage opposite the Lamb Inn belonging to the Planks family which was convenient because one of my mother's jobs was looking after Mrs Plank's daughter. People always seemed to treat us as outsiders, although later when we had a house in Potterne we enjoyed it much more because the people were friendlier.

Boys of the Devizes Grammar School, a small private school in Heathcote House, demonstrate their gymnastic skills, c. 1912.

One of my sisters worked for the Nivens in their house at Marden in the 1930s. At the start of the War some of the wealthier families were finding it difficult to get staff to help them in their houses; the days before the gentry came down to earth! Old Mrs Niven was heard to say. 'I can't get any maids anywhere'. I had done some domestic service but right from a young age I hated it and felt these people were lazy and should do their own work. By then, anyway, I had found a job with a lady at the lodge house at Urchfont Manor who was setting up a goat farm and this was my start with working on farms and with animals, which I enjoyed. Mrs

Niven was so desperate to get anyone to cook for her that when my mother would occasionally agree to help she sent the chauffer-driven car to fetch her! My mother also worked at Urchfont Manor for the Pollock family in the late 1930s where she got two shillings for three hours scrubbing.

Dilys Fell

Michael Hobbs in his pram at the rear of Vales Lane off Sheep Street in 1946. The Baptist chapel is in the background.

A ladies session at Devizes swimming pool in the canal pound near St Peter's School in 1920. The little girl is Kathleen Sanders.

Crystal Set

Our first radio was built by my father. It had accumulators, a crystal and a cat's whisker and we listened to it through earphones. It was one of my jobs to take the accumulators to be recharged by Mr Trotter in Sheep Street. Eventually we got a loudspeaker.

Barbara Wickett

At Home in the High Street

I was born at number 12 in 1895 and then later we moved to number 6 in the High Street. The street for us, when we were children, was the centre of the universe! My father was the manager for F. Bird and Sons, the West Country Coal Merchants and we used the front downstairs room as the office and we had our drawing room upstairs. I enjoyed living in that house and I especially enjoyed the garden. I remember getting up on the wall for the first time and seeing a new world on the other side! When I was older, at about ten years old, I was more adventurous and we would go for walks. We went to Potterne, our farthest point, looked at the old house and went up and down the street, feeling so far from home!

Lillian Hinxman

Gardens in the Breach

Some families who lived in the town and had no garden with the house, rented one on the edge of town. Many of the people who owned Brittox shops rented a garden in the Breach. We had one which had forty-two apple trees! We had a little summer house and went up there in the summer for the day, taking our food with us. This was before most of the houses now in the Breach were built.

Miss Kemp

Devizes' town crier, John Nott takes his turn in the *Daily Express* Town Criers Championship held in the

Market Place in Devizes in 1912.

Kippers

My father used to go down to the station in the morning to pick up boxes of kippers, they came on from Trowbridge, and when I was a boy I used to have to take them round Long Street, Bridewell Street, Hare and Hound Street, selling them from the boxes. The kippers were a penny a pair then. My father had a rhyme that he used to say :

> Aye, aye, aye,
> Kippers penny a pair,
> Bloaters three for tuppence,
> You can buy them anywhere.
> The cheapest shop in London,
> Is down the Old Kent Road,
> When you walk by,
> You get a black eye
> And a punch on top of the nose!

After I'd helped with the fish my next job was with Hampton's Dairy. I delivered milk for the Castle, then I went up to The Brittox where I polished the brass name plate at Bawn's chemists, she paid me threepence for that, and then I went to school.

Charlie Stevens

Town Criers Contest

In 1912 there was a national competition for town criers which was held in Devizes. I was very small then but I remember worming my way through the crowd which packed the Market Place to see the goings on. The main events took place from a podium placed in front of the Bear Hotel at the bottom of the steps leading up to the revolving doors and also in front of the Shambles. The trees in the Market Place were always very useful for gaining a better view of things happening there. I climbed into them to watch bands playing and other events when I was young. A military band on its way from Devizes station to a camp on Salisbury Plain stayed in the town for two or three days and played in the Market Place.

Leonard Strong

A Ride on the Laundry

Our house backed up to the houses in St John's Alley and there was a lady who lived there and did the washing for the Town School. At this time my sisters, who were ten years older than me, were at the school and sometimes, when the washing was being delivered to the school, I would have a ride on the top of the laundry as it was taken back on a cart! My sisters were often late for school, although they would leave home in High Street at eight o'clock to get to Sheep Street for nine! On one of my trips to the school I saw them sitting one in each corner of the classroom wearing the dunce's caps.

Violet Scudamore

Bread and Potatoes

My mother was a good plain cook, there was no nonsense about it. She had a sister who was a vegetarian and so my mother decided we would be vegetarians and we didn't patronise the butcher Mr Godfrey anymore but more

A charabanc trip to Weymouth from St Peters Church in 1919. Young Jack Fell sits at the front with his mother.

Simpson's grocery in the Market Place. Very dignified Mr Godfrey was and a Quaker. I had potatoes, as I didn't like other vegetables and my mother had no idea about food values so I was allowed to have mashed potatoes with butter as often as I liked. I don't remember having much else for a long time, except bread. We ate Bermaline bread from Strongs, a very superior sort of brown bread, for breakfast, dinner and tea, which we ate with Hampton's butter. There were two Strong's shops; big Strongs in The Brittox and Little Strongs in The Little Brittox. I also remember a baker in Northgate Street who had two thumbs on one hand. He would come out of his shop to take the air and stand by the door wearing his voluminous white apron and a baker's cap.

Lillian Hinxman

A Workhouse Boy

My grandmother was returning from shopping one day in 1933 when she passed a group of inmates from the Devizes Workhouse out on their exercise walk. They were brought out at a set time everyday and they walked in crocodiles, one of boys and men and one of girls and women. When she got home she told us that she was sure that she had recognised one of her grandsons with them! We decided to wait until my

31

A view down Caen Hill in the peaceful days of the 1950s. The house on the right was built by Rendells as a 'show house' and the girder railway bridge was removed in 1966 when the branch line closed.

father came home from work and to decide then what to do. When he came home he said that if she was sure that it was him then we should go down there straight away and get him out. We went to the workhouse and picked him out and after arrangements had been made he came home to live with us. He was about fifteen but as he didn't have a birth certificate and didn't know how old he was we had to choose a birthday for him. My grandmother said that we should pick 11 November 1918 as that was a day to celebrate, it being the day the War finished, so that became his birthday. I can't remember how long he had been living in workhouses but we found out how he had come to be there. He had been brought up in South Wales and my family had not seen him for a long time. When his mother died his

father had chosen to keep his sister with him but to admit Garry to the local workhouse. The workhouse only gave support to people who were born in the parish so eventually he was sent to Devizes because he was born in Chirton. He had arrived in a hopeless state and didn't know us. He was not used to people being nice to him and it was a long time before he settled down. He was confused and cried a lot at first. He took a long time to get used to being offered food or drink when it wasn't a meal time. He joined the army when he was eighteen but stayed with us until he got married. We became his family.

Elsie Watts

A Workhouse Visit

I always hated the workhouse. As a young girl I once went with my mother to visit an old person she knew who lived there. All the people were sitting in a row round the side of the room and the lady that we had come to see said she was thirsty. I knew where there was a tap so I went to get her a drink of water. Just as I was giving it to her one of the staff knocked the cup from my hand! We were told that it was not yet time for them to have drinks and that she would be given one later.

Maudie Dunford

Home in Estcourt Terrace

When my father died my mother was left with five of us to bring up and there was no widow's pension in those days. My mother got no money from the business although my grandfather still ran it and his father had before him. We lived in Estcourt Terrace and I went to Southbroom School opposite St James' church.

My mother began to take in lodgers and one day a teacher from Southbroom School, Mr Cozens, came to ask if we had any spare rooms. He had been a science teacher at Dauntsey's School and we recognised him because when he taught there he had walked to school from Devizes and we used to see him going past our house every day. He had one of our rooms when one became free and his married daughter and her little boy stayed as well for a time, while her husband, who was a sailor, was at sea. He only worked at Southbroom School

Florence Chivers with baby Gwen in 1917. The photograph was taken in the Sidmouth Street studio by John Chivers who was Florence's brother-in-law.

for about two years before he decided to start up on his own. He had lost his job at Dauntsey's only a few years before his pension was due and he had little money, having cared for his first wife who had died after a long illness. Doctors' fees were expensive before the National Health Service.

When he came to stay with us he had everything he owned in a tin trunk. He started the Devizes School of Commerce with Mr Smith which was initially in Long Street. Later my mother and he got married and so he became my stepfather.

Gwen Chivers

A Sunday School group from the old Baptist chapel in 1929, photographed by Mr Ashworth in his studio in Maryport Street. Gwen Chivers, age 12 years, is sitting on the left.

Police Headquarters

The old police headquarters was in the Bath Road where High Lawns is now. I remember that this was a considerable building and that bloodhounds were kept there which could be seen in a run. They were a great interest to us as we went by on our walks. I don't remember ever seeing them being used but they were taken out for exercise.

Leonard Strong

Miss Dalloway

Miss Dalloway was the sister of Mr Figgins the grocer and she had a reputation for helping poor people of the town. On Sundays 'her boys', all ragamuffins, would crowd in to her in a room she had in Maryport Street where she gave them a good tea. When their shoes were worn out she'd manage to find them a pair or a shirt if she could. She was the brightest little soul, we would go to see her on Saturday mornings and she was like the sun, always beaming!

Lillian Hinxman

Roundway Hospital Patients

As a child I saw great processions of patients from Roundway Hospital being taken on walks around the town. They walked in crocodiles and were accompanied by uniformed staff.

Leonard Strong

Friends and neighbours in the garden of Jeffrey's Court, at the rear of Ivy House, *c.* 1946. Front row, left to right: Janet Hiscock, Ruth Underwood, Elaine Hiscock, Doreen Underwood, Ken Hillier. Back row: Margaret Giddings, Tony Giddings, Bill Underwood, Donald Gee.

Church and Chapel

My father was a non-Conformist and came from a Baptist family and mother was Church. My father wouldn't go into a church, unless it was for a wedding or a funeral, but he generously allowed mother to bring us up as Church of England. As a treat for him sometimes I would go with him to chapel but I didn't like it very much. Father sang in the choir, it was all very hearty but I don't remember where I sat, perhaps with the ladies in the choir. I went to sleep in one of the long sermons and when I woke up I found everyone was smiling at me. I wasn't very keen on the chapel, I found the Church more entertaining! At first we went to St James' because we lived near it but later,

after we moved house, we went to St John's and then later still, because there was a very old rector at St John's and the services were very boring, we went St Mary's. I remember being very confused at St James', as a young child, on hearing the people singing, 'Praise Him and magnify Him for ever', when I couldn't see anyone with a glass or any other means of 'magnifying' the rector, who I thought the words must refer to, except perhaps those who were wearing glasses! I wasn't impressed with them!

Olive Chivers

Skating on the Crammer in *c.* 1953. In this line-up are, from left to right: 'Weasel' Jones, Stan Laurel, 'Boss' Russell, Roy Palmer, Ken Palmer, 'Bonk' Davis.

Playing in the Workshop

My uncle was John Chivers and he died when I was about eight. I can remember playing with his son Colin, who was about my age, at the shop in Sidmouth Street. The shop was next to Raddon's funeral parlour, a greengrocers called Skiptrells, which was next to a mens' clothiers run by Harry Ellen. We used to go right out to the back to play in the studio or the carpentry workshop where they made the coffins and other things and where my father worked. We would pile up some shavings and sawdust at the bottom of the stairs and jump into them from a few steps up. We used to climb into the coffins too, especially when my father wanted to measure one up for a child who was about my size!

Gwen Chivers

CHAPTER 2

Schools and schooldays

Class IVa of the Secondary School in July 1933 in the garden of Braeside which was used by the school as an extension for classes and other activities.

The Secondary School in Bath Road, c. 1929. This school was opened in 1906 and later became St Peter's School after secondary pupils moved to the newly formed Grammar School on the Green.

Devizes' Little Schools

There were many schools in Devizes before the last war and there was a lot of scope for small private schools, created partly by the demands of local farmers. A lot of farmers in the area didn't want their children to go the village school and so they sent them to Devizes to board during the week at one of the many little schools. Many of these were in quite little houses, Long Street had several. Verecroft School was in the house opposite the entrance to Bridewell Street and the Devizes School of Commerce was on the same side a little further up. This one was later in Estcourt Street in a part of Mr Cozen's house. Wilsford House School was also in Long Street, opposite the top of Hillworth Road. One of the cottages in London Road, just on the right after the bridge, was a tiny boarding school. Parnella House school started in Long Street before it moved to the Market Place.

Olive Chivers

A Variety of Schools

Initially we had a governess and were taught at home - pothooks, elementary things, and so on. Then we went to a private school, Heathcote House on the Green, run by Miss Pugh. Her brother had a boarding school for boys, Devizes Grammar School, which was adjacent to it. Miss Pugh's school was a dame school and it was of quite a substantial size, all the young children of the town's best-known families went to Miss Pughs. I was about five when I went there and later graduated to the Grammar School. A lot of the local children went there, including children of farming families. When Miss Pugh got older she gave up the school and it was taken over by some people called Thurnam who, I believe, did not run it so well. The Secondary School in the Bath Road, opposite Shane's Castle, was a very good school, it opened around the turn of the century and children from all the neighbouring areas went there. Children from the villages came in by bicycle and you could take your meals there.

There were a lot of schools in Devizes at the time. Parnella House in the

St Peter's infants school in 1920.

Market Place was a school and opposite this was Miss Bennet's College where all the boys had scarlet caps. They were known as the 'college boys'. Rumsey's School was where the Conservative Club is now in Long Street. This school had a gymnasium and this was used by the boys from the Grammar School as well. I can remember going there. Eastcroft House was also a school at one time.

I can't recall myself being very good at school but I can remember being presented with a book by Miss Pugh for being the 'best boy in the school'. It was a natural history book called *Lives of the Fur Folk,* it had Redpad the Fox, Grimalkin the cat and Stubs the Badger. If your parents paid for it you used to get two biscuits and a glass of milk in the breaktime. My parents did not want to pay for us to have this but I discovered that when it was breaktime and all the children used to gather round for the distribution of Osborne or Marie biscuits, if I went to the back and put my hand up I would also get two biscuits!

Leonard Strong

The 'Best' Schools

I went to Parnella School first, which was one of a succession of private schools at the time. The well-to-do tradesmen sent their children to Miss Bennett's school, the Devizes College in St Johns Street, but we went to Parnella House because it was a bit cheaper! When Miss Bennett's closed I remember that in the *Advertiser*, an old paper which was published by Gillmans in The Brittox, someone called it his alma mater and had such a veneration for it but I don't know that the education was so superior, I expect it was about the same as all the rest of us got! I wrote

39

The Convent School, Bath Road, c. 1927.

endless compositions which, I suppose, must have done me some good. I was taught by Miss Davies and she must have had some success with me because when I transferred to the new Devizes Secondary School, which opened just in time for me when I was eleven and a quarter years old, I was put in the second form. The new school's headmaster ruled us with a rod of iron but he had his mellow moments. Unfortunately, I was very bad in his subjects: my heart always failed me when I got into the lab', I knew that if I was doing an experiment and it was supposed to end with a reduced weight of something, mine would always end with an added weight! I think that I must have been a bit of a nuisance at school; once, against the rules, we stayed after school and played about on the gym apparatus. One of the masters who was taking detention came in and told us not to do it and to go home. We went on; I climbed on a bar

to do a turn or something and fell and broke my collar bone. I wasn't popular for this! Each term we had an exam and if you managed to struggle through you had a merit holiday. For one of these the senior mistress took us for a walk around Roundway during which I saw a dog in a kennel by the roadside and put my hand practically in its mouth. It bit me and I was not popular for that either!

Lillian Hinxman

First Impressions

I went to Southbroom School, opposite the church, and remember on my first day, we slept in the afternoon on wooden trestles. A boy called Michael Star cried all the way through.

When George VI was crowned in 1937 all the school children in Devizes

40

were presented with Coronation books by the mayor. In the days before the presentation we had to rehearse for it at school. Miss Marchant made us line up and I stood with my friend Bernie Bishop, who started school on the same day as me, and as she was saying, 'I want you to imagine that I am the mayor', she felt a sneeze coming on and, as we all watched, she hoisted up her skirt and pulled a handkerchief from her bloomers and blew her nose! I remember saying to Bernie, 'I don't think the mayor would do that'.

Bill Underwood

The Umbrella

Alec Weekes went to the Grammar School and one wet day he came to school with an umbrella and he had hardly got inside the door into the playground of the school when all the boys, mainly the boarders, set on him like a pack of hounds and there was nothing left of the umbrella when school started. They all had to bring four pence in to school to buy a new umbrella!

Leonard Strong

Devizes School of Commerce

My step-father was in his sixties when he began to run the School of Commerce in Long Street with Mr Smith. He ran the school for twenty-one years and retired when he was 87 years old in 1946. He parted company with Mr Smith after only a few years and moved the school into our house at

Advertisement for the Devizes School of Commerce in 1933.

5, Estcourt Terrace. He saved all the money earned from the school to buy our house. I don't think he really charged very much for the fees and never made as much money as he could have done. I went to the school when I was eight and stayed until I was sixteen.

When I left I tried to get a job but there was a shortage of jobs for junior office girls and so I helped my mother at home for a while and then I went back to the school and started teaching there in 1934. I started with some of the young ones, teaching them the ABC the old-fashioned way with the letters and sounds. Up to the age of nine I taught them compositions, spelling and arithmetic, with all kinds of money

Southbroom Senior School, now Devizes School, from the playing field, in c. 1927.

sums, but not fractions, they did that when they went upstairs. No-one taught me to teach, I just did it in the way I had been taught myself. I had one little girl who used to scream and carry on and I put her behind the blackboard and told her, 'The sooner you stop that the sooner you can sit down'.

I used to get them doing all the noisy things in the morning like spelling and dictation and in the afternoons quiet things like copying, drawing and writing, that worked very well. They started the commercial subjects at about eight and learned typing and shorthand. I got my first shorthand certificate before I was eleven.

Gwen Chivers

Mr Cozens' School

Mr Cozens, the head of the school, was a real character, he should have been an actor. He used to read to us on certain days, I particularly enjoyed him reading *Brimsquire* to us, he used to act the part rather than read it to us. He made it live! He also arranged some marvellous trips from the school. We went to Fry's at Bristol and saw chocolate being made and we went to Swindon and the GWR works. We saw the *George V* engine being made.

I once got kept in at school as a punishment. After a long time I plucked up courage and crept downstairs and found that he had forgotten me! It was nearly seven o'clock, he had been to his allotment after school! No-one had thought to look for me because it was summer and I was often out playing with friends till late.

Mr Cozens was a keen gardener and had allotments at Pans Lane and on the London Road where the police headquarters is now. The children at his school all had a little plot which we were taken to visit and look after. I

The Old Woman Who Lived in a Shoe by children at Smith's School in Long Street, *c.* 1925. The characters are, from the left, standing: Violet Scudamore (Polly), Connie Pannel (spider), -?- (Miss Muffet), Henry Furnell (Little Boy Blue), Gwennie Chivers (Little Bo-Peep), Jimmie Few (Little Jack Horner), Hector Hobbs (Jack) and Gwennie Gould (Jill). Sitting in the middle is Olive Chivers, as the Old Woman.

don't think I ever grew much on mine, I didn't like gardening and still don't!

Mr ('Jimmy') Knapman was a teacher at the School of Commerce. He taught copperplate handwriting and I used to get prizes for my writing. People aren't taught to write properly now. He was a tartar about spellings too; we had lists of twenty or thirty words to learn and then we were tested. We were kept in for five minutes for each one we got wrong. There was no speaking during classes and when the teacher came in we stood up. As it was a commercial school we were taught typing and shorthand from an early age. I started shorthand at eight years old.

Violet Scudamore

Kindergarten in Long Street

I went first of all to Parnella House school in the Market Place in the early 1920s and then moved to Long Street, to the kindergarten department of the School of Commerce. I think we were moved when Parnella House changed hands and the fees went up! Quite a lot of children moved at the same time. When we went to start at Long Street we asked what 'kindergarten' meant, it was written up on the wall by the door. I was surprised to find that we were now 'kindergarten', at my first school, we were just known as the 'little ones'. The Long Street school had nowhere to play at all, there was only a little yard at the back and so in the mornings we had to go out for a walk

43

Children and teachers from Devizes School of Commerce in Castle Walk, *c.* 1929. Mr Cozens, the head, is at the back on the right and Miss Lois Drew, a teacher, is in front of him. Mrs Cozens is at the back on

the left and among the pupils are several characters that are well known in town today.

Mr Cozens after his retirement from a long life in teaching, at his home 5, Estcourt Terrace.

and in the afternoons we used fields hired by the school. There was one in Hillworth Road at one time, where the bungalows are now, and also we had one for a time in Hartfield and then one in Nursteed Road.

Our usual route for the morning walk was to come out of the school and turn up Long Street and then down Hillworth Road, or Gallow's Ditch as it was known, to the pond at the end. The pond was surrounded by posts and the boys always ran on ahead to position themselves between the posts and stop the girls from getting through. We would try to push our way through and one day one of the boys was pushed into the pond! The pond was covered in green slime. I remember that Gwennie Chivers and I were walking together, I shall never forget that day. I've always been grateful for those walks, I used to like poking about in the hedges and ditches and it started an interest that stayed with me the rest of my life - so much nicer than just 'going out to play'. Hillworth Road then was like a country lane with houses on just one side.

Olive Chivers

Reverend Billy Weekes

I went to Heathcote House then to the Grammar School. We went down to St Peter's for scripture with Billy Weekes. He was a case! He had a little harmonium and the kids used to play him up and he got so mad. Once he ended up having a tug-o-war across his harmonium with someone he was tryng to catch! He was chaplain at the prison - he should have been in there himself, he was mad! Miss Paradise taught P.E. and on her first day she came in a gym dress much to everyone's amusement. We had carol concerts at Braeside at Christmas organised by Haydn Howells. They were very good.

Peggy Hancock

The Cane

I went to the Town School in Sheep Street when I was little. Some children always tried to take a horse hair to school with them in case they got into trouble. If you were to get the cane for doing something wrong you wound the hair round and round your hand and hoped that the teacher didn't see it. When she gave you a wack on the hand the hair stopped it from hurting and it sometimes split the cane!

Maudie Dunford

Silkworms

When I first went to school I went to Miss Pugh's at Heathcote House on the Green. In the summer we had lessons outside. In the garden was a mulberry tree and we kept silkworms which fed on the mulberry leaves. We kept them in boxes and they spun little cocoons. I started at the school when I was about six and a half as my father had taught me until then. On my first day I spent some of my time teaching the smaller ones and when my father heard this he complained that he hadn't sent me there to teach the others! I was at the school until I was eleven years old after which I went away to school in Weston-super-Mare.

Miss Kemp

Scarlet Fever

I started at Southbroom School opposite the Green church when I was about three years old. Miss Marchant the headmistress used to come into our shop and she was always on to my mother to bring me into school even though I had injured my foot in an accident riding on the back of my father's bike. I can remember being pushed down to the school in a push chair and

Town School for girls and infants in Sheep Street photographed here in the early 1960s but not used as a school since before the war.

sitting in school with my foot up! By the time I was seven I could read and write as well as anybody. Then I went over the Green to Southbroom Senior when I was seven, or rather seven and three months, because I was late starting there. I was up in London while my brother was born, they sent me out of the way to my mother's people, where I caught scarlet fever and I was in hospital for a month. About three weeks after I came back my two cousins that I'd been staying with both caught diphtheria and one of them died. That was in 1927.

Joyce Rose

A Young Naturalist Spurned

When I started school we lived in Dyehouse Lane and I walked to Southbroom School across two fields, through a wood and along a path next to the cemetery and over the canal bridge. I usually walked alone because no-one else lived down our lane and my brothers were much younger than me. I enjoyed school until one day the head-

Staff of Southbroom Secondary Modern school at the rear of the main building in 1948. They are, back row, left to right: Jim Newland, E. Evans, A. Bernard, L. Lowries, N. Fursman, A. Ball. Middle row: J. Duderidge, E. Palmer, M. Pearce, M. Garratt, A. Street, D. Underwood (Sec.). Front row: -?-, M. Kilroy, S. Prismall, A. Reynolds (Head), Mr Busby, W. McGunnigle, J. Foxhall.

master said something to me that changed my whole attitude to it, and to learning, for a long time.

We didn't have many books in our house when I was a child but there was one that I read and really enjoyed. I could read, by the way, before I went to school, my mother taught me. The book was *Girl of the Limberlost* by Jean Stratton Porter. It was, I suppose, a romantic novel but it contained some descriptions of giant American moths which caught my imagination as a young child. Something that increased this interest, was a story my grandfather told of Mr Tull who kept a shoe shop in The Brittox and had bred giant Himalayan moon moths in an old chapel in his garden, the biggest he had ever seen. Through my grandfather's interest I became mad about moths, wildflowers and birds, which I knew a lot about as a child, and thought I want-ed to do something in that line one day.

When Mr Wesley, the headmaster, came to us that day he asked us what we would like to do when we left school, I said I wanted to be a naturalist. I don't suppose for one moment that he intend-ed the effect his response had on me, but in those days, there were still some people who thought it was wrong to educate children to have ideas above their station and he thought, perhaps, that by this he was doing me a service, when he absolutely scorned my reply to the whole class. He said I had ridiculous ideas, that naturalists were clever people who wrote books and it was silly to think that I could ever do that. It flat-tened me and I abandoned all interest in nature study and lost my confidence to write anything for a long time.

Arthur Cleverly

The girls of the Devizes School of Commerce photographed outside the door in Estcourt Terrace, *c.* 1937.

Girls from Devizes Secondary School in the Bath Road photographed at Braeside in about 1933. Second from the right on the back row is Joyce (Rose) Buckland.

Olive Chivers, Mary Waight and Kitty Bolwell walking home from the Secondary School in the Bath Road in 1933.

School Walks

On one particular day in the winter I remember our walk was supervised by the French mistress. We came down through St John's churchyard and up the path to Gallow's Ditch, where the pond was frozen. The mistress was quite a young filly and had a fur coat on. As we got to the pond we were joking about someone falling in and no sooner had we said it than Ralph Chivers fell in! After he had been fished out he was the envy of everyone because he got the French mistress's fur coat to wear back to school! Hillworth Road was only a small roadway then with very little building in it and we regularly used to have nature walks along the hedgerows.

Violet Scudamore

Squeaky Slates

My first school was Southbroom by St James Church and when I first went there, there were infants, juniors and senior departments. I used a slate when I started, it was very squeaky! I have a vivid memory of my first school, we used to do knitting, even when we were only five and I used to hate it. We had some red wool and we had to knit a long strip like a scarf but with every line it got wider, the teacher was so annoyed, and then I dropped the ball of wool and it got all tangled round the iron legs of the desk. I was crying as I tried to untangle it while the teacher stood over me! I left there when I was six.

Gwen Chivers

Gym Slips and Stockings

At eleven I went to the Secondary School in Bath Road and I can remember stopping on the way there to watch coal barges on the canal going under the bridge. We wore gym-slips in the winter and pink dresses in the summer. You could choose which uniform you wore in the summer but ankle socks could only be worn with the dresses so if you wore the gym-slip you had to wear stockings. I didn't like the dresses very much, they had white cord stuff all down the front. Some classes were at Braeside and we walked in crocodile between the buildings. There were special places where we had to cross the road depending on which direction we were going in.

Joyce Rose

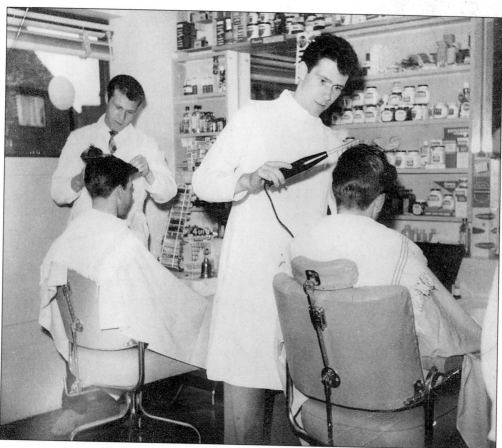

David and Bill Underwood at work in the new shop in 1958 which was built on the site of their father's old shop after the extensive refurbishments of Sheep Street in the 1950s. The other shops in the row at the time were Bessie Pinchin's sweet shop, Bert Maslen's shoe repairs and Arthur Deane's wet fish shop.

The Avon Vale Hounds meet outside the Bear Hotel 12 November 1912.

The Gazette Office

When I finished at the Secondary School in 1936 I worked for about six months in the Co-op but I hated that and then I was offered a job at the *Gazette* office. I did all sorts of office things, typing, accounts and so on. One of my jobs, once a week, was writing out all the cheques which had to be done in the office of Mr Stone, the manager.

Every Thursday morning, which was publishing morning, I had to be in at half past six in order to read the proofs of all the advertisements as these were considered a lot more important than the reading matter. If you had a mistake in an advertisement you could be refused payment! It was printed on the premises. I used to watch the pages coming off the machine which assembled the paper as well. It went to press about mid-morning and then there was the big rush to get the papers out onto the streets and round to the newsagents in the afternoon. They also produced a Saturday paper called the *Advertiser* which had to be got out fairly early because we closed at midday on a Saturday. There was also a printing works there for customer printing which was run by Gerry Gosling. Our head-office was in Swindon, The *North Wilts*

"How's Trade John?"

"Slack, the worst patch I've struck in years. Money's getting tight, you know."

"Why not advertise?"

"Yes, but how? I've never bothered about it before."

"Well, I've found that newspaper advertisements bring the best results, and for Devizes & District the obvious choice is the

Wiltshire Gazette

Selling 1½ copies for every household in the borough.
★ Total county sales in excess of 15,300 copies weekly.

An advertisement for the *Wiltshire Gazette*, 1956.

Anstie's factory offices in the Market Place in the 1950s.

Herald, and the accountant used to come over to us occasionally and we made our returns to them. Although I was straight from school I had to keep all the records of sales, percentages and so on, on great sheets of paper. I was better at handling decimals and things than anyone else in the office! One day someone came round selling slide rules, which I had learned to use at school, and I persuaded them to buy one for me. When I left, the slide rule had to stay behind even though no-one in the office knew how to use it!

I was given a lot of responsibility in the *Gazette* office but because I was very young I wasn't paid very well for it. I was complaining about this one day to one of the senior reporters who knew someone who worked at W.E. Chivers. He offered to speak to them for me and try to get me a better paid job there. When my mother got to hear of this she said that I couldn't possibly do that because there would be far too much swearing in the office at Chivers!

Barbara Wickett

Anstie's Factory

After the war I came out of the army and went to work at Anstie's, I was storekeeper in Long Stores. My father worked there as well. Cigarette manufacture was done on the ground floor, that's where the cigarette and packet machines were, and a conveyor belt carried the packets up to the first floor to be packed. Cigarettes had been packed in there since at least before the First World War and inbetween the floor boards you could find dried up old packets of cigarettes. The spaces between the boards were also packed full of chaff

A scene in the stripping room of Anstie's tobacco factory in about 1920.

because the building had been used at one time as a fodder store. The buildings at the Market Place end were just offices. The upper floors of Long Stores end were used for storage, packing materials mainly, and it was the only place where there was a power lift. It was only for goods though, you loaded it up and then chased up the stairs to unload it.

There was a very large cellar with an old well. The top of the well was bricked around in a cone shape with the hole in the middle. It was used for years for dumping rubbish in, old broken glass and so on, it didn't matter how much you put in, it always sank down eventually. After the war all the drill materials from the home guard, including old grenades, were dumped down there. Anstie's threw away a lot of their old dies for cigarette printing down there too, they made cigarettes for other companies and didn't want these to get into the hands of anyone else. One day I was down the cellar on my own and throwing down it some old, broken glass plates used as window advertisements for tobacco, Brown Beauty and Black Beauty, and it was taking a long time for them to go down. To speed it up I climbed in to the top of the well and jumped up and down on the glass which made it suddenly drop about five feet! Luckily, I was able to catch the top of the brick edge just in time to prevent myself slipping down with it.

Tobacco arrived as dry leaf in hogsheads. These were big cylindrical containers about four to five feet long and made of wood. Nearly all the tobacco came from India although it was all called 'Virginia'. Some came from Africa. They arrived from the station on lorries and were pushed off the end and rolled in through big double doors in New Street [Snuff Street]. The leaves were unpacked and taken to the wetting down room where they were moistened then spread out on big tables for stripping. Removing the stalk was known as stripping and this was done by hand, mainly by the girls. There were always jokes about the girls in the 'stripping off room'. After this the tobacco went to the cutting room where it was cut up in high speed machines for the tobacco and for cigarettes. The big sellers for a while were Anstie's Gold Flake and Anstie's Cambridge. We also made cigarettes for I. Rutter & Co. who had been in Mitcham and for them we made Tobaccao Bloom which was a more expensive cigarette. The owner of Rutters lived at Potterne.

We had a weekly allowance of twenty free cigarettes and we could buy more at a reduced price. Practically everyone smoked in those days and most people who had been in the army during the war came out as smokers.

Arthur Cleverly

First Job

Mr Dewsnap was the manager at Anstie's factory during the war. He was a Londoner and used to wear a bowler hat, black jacket and striped trousers. He walked briskly through the factory at a certain time each morning, saying, 'Good morning' as he went. He lived in Pans Lane. There was another old toff, a director, who used to walk through as well and he would always pick up some tobacco and sniff it on his way through, it was a ritual with him. When I went for the job I had to see Mr Dewsnap. He just checked that my hands were alright, that I hadn't got any skin disease or anything and I got the job. It was wartime and people were being called up, I was fourteen and a half.

Ralph Merrett

Wadworths

I started at the brewery in 1934 to learn brewing and malting. In those days Wadworths had its own maltings which were where Kennet House is at the top of Station Road. We bought local barley

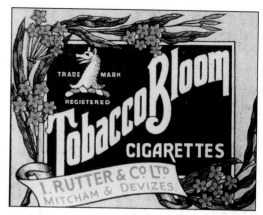

A packet of twenty cigarettes made by Ansties for the firm of I. Rutter, c. 1950.

for malting. In 1939 when the war started I was one of a minority of males left in the town because as I was involved here as a brewer, and we supplied beer to the local camps, I was exempt from service. During the war most of the staff in the brewery were women and they operated many of the processes, including washing the casks and the fermenting vessels.

In my earlier days with the firm we had a large private trade sale, about 3,000 customers, as well as the free trade and tied pubs. Many of the private customers were farmers. Before the war we had a wider range of beers: there was 6X, 4X, 2X and Harvest Ale which was a light beer brewed in the summer that farmers bought to give to their workers. Then there was P.A. and I.P.A.

Gordon Bertwistle

Errand Boy at the Brewery

I began at Wadworths in January 1938 at the age of fifteen. I would start work at a quarter to six in the morning

Head Brewer at Wadworths, Peter Wilson, checks the specific gravity in a fermenting vessel, 1960s.

by calling at the post office to collect the mail in a leather bag. The men in the yard would be waiting for me before starting to check off the empties, the beer barrels, beer crates, AWs (aerated waters) and soft drinks bottles from the lorry, brought back the previous day. At half past eight was the breakfast break and I used to go home for breakfast and come back at half past nine, finish that job at about eleven and then go into the office. Then I'd go round and take orders from all the staff for dodgers (bread rolls) and cheese and go to the Pelican and buy them. They cost three-pence each then, the old threepence. Then after that I'd take the orders for cigarettes and tobacco from all the staff

and cycle up to Anstie's and get that. I saw Mr Wally Abrams in the retail shop at the New Park Street end of the factory and then I'd come back with orders of Players, Capstain Full Strength, tobacco and cigars and go into my little office on the corner of the brewery, which is still there, and make out an invoice for each person and get the money. No-one was allowed to smoke in the brewery while they were working, they were very strict about that.

In the afternoons I had to deliver the mail but first I put all the letters through a sort of press to make copies of them and then put them into envelopes, there'd be about fifty letters. All the letters were typed by an old man called Mr Stanlyforth. I finished work at half past five in those days but after work I would have to deliver any local letters, which took me about an hour. At this time I used to get a bicycle allowance of one pound every three months, which was very good because you could buy a bicycle for about three pounds and my wages were only 5/- a week which came down to 4/8d after the deduction for my insurance stamp. I got my first increase after I had been there for a year, Mr Jacky Bartholomew, Major Bartholomew's father, put his hand on my shoulder one day and said in a whisper, 'you are the best office boy we've ever had and we are going to increase your wages by fifty percent'. That was half a crown extra making me up to 7/2d in the old money - marvellous! We worked very hard for this though, including Saturday morning until one o'clock. Working conditions were very strict too - if you wanted to go to the toilet you had to catch the head clerk's eye and ask his permission. If you weren't back in two minutes -

A group of Wadworth's staff in the yard holding the new company flag in 1975. Two people in the picture are still employed at the brewery in 1996, they are Gloria Tucker (Grant), right of centre, and Andy Underwood, extreme right. Ron Tumber, third from left, joined the company as brewery foreman in 1950.

look out!

Cecil Scratchley

Gas Street Lamps

In the 1940s the street lights were mainly gas and I remember that a man came along each week to our shop in Maryport Street and put his ladder up against the wall. He climbed the ladder to a little handle and wound down a steel wire that held the gas lamp over the middle of the road, between our building and Neates, where Tesco is now. Then he stood in the middle of the road and cleaned the glass and changed the mantle. Although the traffic was two-way in those days he was rarely interrupted and he did this every week!

Chris Bush

Bath Road looking towards Prison Bridge in about 1924.

Chivers' Apprentices

After school I was apprenticed at Chivers on the steam engines when I was fourteen years old. In the 1930s Chivers were still heavily involved with steam power. I got five shillings a week which went down to three and tenpence after insurance. I gave it all to my mother and she gave me back a shilling. I couldn't afford to drink or smoke but I usually went to the pictures each week. My father was a foreman bricklayer with Chivers and had started with the firm right at the beginning. I learned welding on the fire-boxes, at that time no-one else did any welding there. I did some amateur box-ing in my spare time, sometimes doing three fights in one day. We trained at the Territorial Army Drill Hall.

I was with Chivers for about five years but when I finishd my apprentice-ship I didn't want to stay any longer, after all that low pay, so I went up to Birmingham and worked for Brightside Engineering. I stayed with them right up to the War and then stayed to work on tanks and aircraft. I welded manifolds on damaged Spitfire engines using old hacksaw blades and borax which was all we had to do it with.

Much later I had my own workshop in Devizes, it was up the side of the Candy Store where the old slaughter house used to be. The iron rings in the floor where the cattle were held are still there now, as far as I know. I remember when I was a boy seeing a young bull come charging out of there and run off up towards the assize courts where he got himself caught on the railings. Later I moved to the workshop in Lower Wharf by the canal, behind Wadworths. I made all sorts of ironwork, gates and brackets and my work can still be seen all over town. I made a new lantern for outside the Artichoke inn. The original one was made of lead and was badly worn, I think they still have the old one at the back somewhere.

Jack Fell

W.E. Chivers' sawmills in Nursteed Road in about 1918.

I had always been mad on engineering, I had passed my engineering badge in the scouts and I wanted to get a job at Chivers but to get an apprenticeship in those times you had to be able to pay a premium and if you had poor parents you didn't have the money for it. I was brought up by my grandparents and I used to worry them about this apprenticeship although I think at the time I didn't understand about the money that was needed. There were certain charities available to support apprentices if you could get one and my grandfather must have spoken to someone about this because he suddenly changed his mind about me getting into Chivers and said that if I could get the job they would see to the premium. He had managed to set me up with The Broad Town Charity who had agreed to apprentice me if I could get a job. I then set about getting one but each time I went along to Estcourt Street to see Mr Harry Chivers he was always busy or was not there. Eventually the time came when he was there and all he asked me was who my father was. I told him my grandfather's name and he said, 'Oh yes, that will be alright' and so I began.

Ralph Merrett

Delivery Boy

My first job was with the New Era Laundry in Sheep Street. I was a delivery boy but I didn't do the driving, someone else did that. It was heavy lifting work and I was only small. One day the man from Walker's Stores in The Brittox asked me if I would work for them as a delivery boy. 'Will you pay me more than I am getting now,' I asked him and he said, 'yes', so I changed jobs.

Charlie Stevens

Jack Fell in his workshop at Lower Wharf completing a new lantern for the Artichoke Inn in the mid 1970s.

The View from the Brewery

I started work at Wadworths in 1947 as a short-hand typist in an office with a window overlooking the corner opposite. I typed up all the letters each day and then copied them in an old press that I believe is still there. There were no filing cabinets in those days so all the correspondence was entered into the letter book which was indexed and that was our filing system.

Sometimes I would look out of the window and down over the rooftops to the small houses and shops on the corner, all gone now. I remember that I could see the ladies coming and going in the courts around these houses, often with their curlers in or a turban on, but I can't remember anyone ever looking up at where I was. I suppose they were so used to the building being there they didn't think. Among the shops on the corner was a bakers, a fruit and vegetables shop called Stones, Harry Oakford's cycle shop, Charlie Figgins' paper shop, later bought by Peter Flippence, and the tobacconists, Weston's, which is still there.

Betty Scratchley

Cellarman

I started at Wadworths in 1950. We came from Faversham in Kent and I had been working from the age of fourteen in breweries. I've worked in practically every department with the exception of the actual brewing itself; in cellars, bottling, packing and the office. I saw the job advertised in the *The Kent Messenger*. The head clerk, who came here just before me, worked at the same brewery in Kent that my brothers worked in and he had put the advert in the paper. I read it and took a chance. The job was for brewery foreman, in charge of cellars. I assisted the brewer, Mr Wilson, to work out the brewing for the following week, which we did each Friday afternoon. We worked hand to mouth. The production in those days was much smaller than it is now, we would work out the week's brewing almost to the last half pint. By Friday afternoon my cellars were empty. The company was not so strong as it is now and I think it actually nearly went down at about this time. It was very hard work and no-one wanted to stop there for

The Bacon Factory football team in c. 1923.

very long at that time. I think we only stayed at first because we wanted to get away from Kent! There were about nine lorries then compared to about twenty now. Trade began to pick up as new people came who had experience of other breweries and modern ideas, but it was very hard work then.

We lived in a house in the yard and I was on twenty-four hour call. If the police saw a light on in the brewery at night they would come and knock my door and get me up to go and check it. I went down there one day with one of them and went in to look round and found a gentleman in there, it was the excise officer. The policeman said, 'What's he doing?', and I said, 'He's entitled to come to this place, twenty-four hours a day, he has his own keys to each department. That's been the rule since I first worked in the breweries. They check to make sure that you're not doing anything that you are not supposed to be doing.

In the 1950s there were beers brewed that are not around now. We had Brown Jack, a strong bottled beer, sold in draught as Old Timer. I think Brown Jack was a race horse. There was an ordinary bitter sold as draught in the pubs and the 6X was sold in bottles as Green Label with only a small amount sold then as draught.

When I started, bottling was done practically all by hand. The girls carried bottles from the big soakers and put them onto a brush machine, with twin brushes, and then into a rinser and then straight to the fillers, all by hand. Seven or eight girls worked all in a row. A machine did the filling, from a tank into about twenty bottles at a time, with a ball valve to stop them overflowing. It was noisy, especially when something went wrong and bottles went crashing everywhere!

Ron Tumber

The road to Devizes under the railway bridge and up Caen Hill. This photograph by Mr Edmonds of High Street was taken in about 1912.

Death at the 'Crown'

Mr Bertwistle, later Wadworth's free trade director, had a call from the landlord of The Crown at Marston one day in the 1940s. The man's wife had died and when the funeral directors arrived to collect her they could not get the coffin down the winding staircase. His wife was a big woman and weighed about twenty-two stones and he wanted permission to remove the upstairs window and lower the coffin into the road! This was eventually done. The Crown is no longer a pub but the building is still there.

Cecil Scratchley

Cycling to Melksham

After leaving school, it was in the early thirties, I started work at the Avon in Melksham. I worked for the chief chemist as his secretary and cycled to work for a while. It was hard work cycling home after a day's work up those hills on my heavy old-fashioned bicycle! Later I worked for Strattons the wholesale grocers in Monday Market Street until the start of the war when I joined the WAAFs.

Violet Scudamore

Snuff Making

The worst job in the factory was snuff making. Anstie's started as snuff

Chivers' carpentry workshop in Estcourt Street in about 1960. Dennis Fowler and Henry Amor are in the foreground.

A quiet Market Day , probably in the 1940s.

The Estcourt Fountain photographed by John Chivers when the water was actually flowing! Most early pictures of it, and this one may be from the late 1880s, show it still.

makers and originally ground it at Calstone Mill and Whistley Mill, near Potterne, because there was no water power in Devizes. Later electrical power allowed them to do it at the Devizes factory and it was made on the second and third floors in the New Street part. Snuff was made from waste tobacco, that included sweepings, any damaged leaf and also returned tobacco sent back by tobacconists as old stock. It was put into the cellar on a stone floor in big heaps, like compost heaps, moistened and kept just like compost, under sacking. When it was deemed to have, well, sort of rotted down enough, it was taken out and dried on great big metal pans heated with steam. When it was completely dry it was fit for milling. It was carried upstairs in sacks to the milling floors. The milling rooms had quite low

ceilings, very little ventilation and no extractors or anything like that because all the profits would be whisked away! No-one wanted to become the snuff maker's assistant and only one man worked as the miller. No-one in their right mind would have wanted his job, even on a hot day all the windows were kept shut to avoid losing any snuff. The milling was done with open grinding wheels and the prepared tobacco was just shovelled into the mills and when they started to grind it was just like a brown fog in the room. No masks were worn and the first time you did it you lasted only about an hour before you had to rush from the room and be very sick. You could feel yourself filling up with snuff, your mouth was coated with it, it was in your ears and nose and clothes. The snuff miller seemed able to

A group of Night Staff entrants for the Roundway Hospital Staff Carnival in *c.* 1956.

stick it but his assistants were always chosen from people who had only just started at the factory and had not yet got a fixed job. You didn't want any food during the day, all I could take was cups of tea.

After the first milling the powder was ground again in special cone-shaped mills that made it even finer. Then it was sifted through a silk screen that vibrated and what came through that was like dust. Some of the snuffs were perfumed. We made a brand called Otto de Rose which was made with pure attar of roses from Bulgaria. This was an oily, waxy substance made from roses that was added to the snuff in small quanti-

ties but after the war it became too expensive to use.

Soon after I started at the factory, the job of storekeeper came up and I got that. I said at the time that I would leave rather than work in the snuff mills again.

Arthur Cleverly

May's Furniture Shop

I worked for May's in Maryport Street after my mother died, doing clerical and typing for a while and then I took over things like wages, insurance

65

Moore and Bush's shop in Maryport Street, c. 1960.

Night Nurse

I worked as a night nurse at Roundway Hospital from 1950 to 1983. At its height in the middle of that period it had over 1,000 people working there including all the medical, maintenance and ground staff. I don't know what the total number of patients was but there were at least 1,000 women when I was there. Some patients had been admitted in the early days for almost nothing at all and were still in-patients. One old lady in her eighties had spent her life there and was admitted because she had had an illegitimate child.

We had our own carnivals and groups of staff dressed up and we made elaborate floats. Sport and music were important things at the hospital, if you could play an instrument or were good at football you were employable! There were some really good music concerts and regular sporting events.

Joyce Rose

Moore and Bush

Originally the business was an electrical contracting one and the shop was really just a place where people came to pay their bills. We had a few things to sell, like radios and other electrical goods but mainly we were involved in supplying private power plants for the big country houses. Locally we supplied Roundway House, Old Park, Broadleas and Oare with electrical plants, but we worked all over the West of England, installing plants to farms and houses. We usually supplied a charging dynamo with a large storage

stamps, accounts and bought ledger. There were about thirty-six on the wages list. May's had two shops in Maryport Street, The Oddfellows' Hall and the building that's opposite the toyshop and is now a building society. There was high class furniture in the hall, with two men assistants, and there were ladies selling materials at the other shop. There was a sewing room where they did the upholstery and they had removal men and carpet and lino layers. On Wednesday it was early closing day and the office girls used to go and look at the furniture in the hall and try out the chairs!

Gwen Chivers

A trade stand for Moore and Bush Ltd with Desmond Perry in attendance, in the Shambles, *c.* 1957.

battery of fifty-four cells which delivered 110 volts DC. We had a big staff of electricians who did all the house wiring. I had trained as a teacher but got involved in this business over the wiring of churches and a dairy when I was in Shrewton. I had learned all about it from reading books and so on, then I met Mr Moore and in 1937 I was invited to manage the Devizes branch of the James Brothers firm which was based in Trowbridge. When the brothers retired in 1946, and I came out of the RAF, we bought the Devizes and Trowbridge businesses, with Mr Moore, and formed Moore and Bush Ltd.

As well as the contracting side and the sales we also charged radio accumulators, in the cellar, for sixpence a time.

Fred Bush

Power Plant Engineers

All factories and works needed their own power plants in the old days. The engineer on site was an important man, he had to keep things running. There was always the unmistakeable noise of a power plant working away somewhere in any factory or works. Sometimes the fuel was town gas, on the smaller ones, but it could be anthracite or could be gas produced on site, in others. Chivers' plant at the sawmills made their own gas fuel by burning waste wood and sawdust. This required gas plant to 'wash' the gas and extract the tar, one of my jobs was to do the tar extraction. Sometimes the power was used as a straight take-off using belt drives, Ansties used those for driving some of their machinery at first, but

Sidmouth Street, looking towards Maryport Street in the 1950s. Albion Place, on the left, still has gardens and beyond Handel House, on the corner of Sheep Street, is E.F. Duck's shop followed by the boys' Town School building and Neate's furniture depository, where Tesco now stands. On the right is T.H.White's shop followed by Wiltshire's on the corner.

generated electricity for other things like the lighting. When I worked at Chivers in Estcourt Street, in the 1940s, I remember that if the lights began to flicker the plant engineers would drop whatever they were doing and dash out to the plant to stoke up the fuel or stir up the gas plant! Anstie's used two Crossley engines and Chivers had at least one Crossley. The Palace cinema had two out at the back. Bigger places had a battery room, as well, to store some power for such as Saturday morning, small jobs.

Ralph Merrett

Hot Pennies

There was a man who worked in the yard at Wadworths as a general help, just after the war, his name was Dick Giddings. He was always hard up and trying to find some money, he lived with his sister who used to take his wage packet and give him back a few pence to last him the week. Each morning when we were checking off the empties coming back in, aerated water and beer bottles, he would be up on the lorry passing the cases to the edge to make it easier for others to check them off at two dozen to a crate, before they were taken off to the various departments. You would often find in the crates a penny or an odd sixpence that had fallen in there at the pub from the till so it was customary to give them a shake to see if they rattled. This character would always be shaking the cases to find any money and when he did he would nearly go beserk because he was so short. There was a fire nearby in a stoke hole

BEERS (in Cask)

	Brl. 36 Gals.	Kil. 18 Gals.	Fir. 9 Gals.	Pin 4½ Gals.
X (Mild)	60/-	30/-	15/-	7/6
XX (Mild)	80/-	40/-	20/-	10/-
XXX (Mild)	96/-	48/-	24/-	12/-
XXXX (Mild)	114/-	57/-	28/6	14/3
6 X (Strong)	154/-	77/-	38/6	19/3
*P.A. (Bitter)	114/-	57/-	28/6	14/3
*I.P.A. (Pale Ale)	130/-	65/-	32/6	16/3
*D.S. (Stout)	114/-	57/-	28/6	16/3

*Specially recommended for Family use.

BEERS (in Bottle)

WADWORTH & Co.'s	Doz. Pts.	Doz. ½-Pts.
India Pale Ale..	—	5/-
Pale Ale		5/-
Home Brewed	7/-	4/-
Oatmeal Stout	7/-	4/-
Brown Ale	7/-	4/-
Amber Ale	6/-	3/3
Strong Ale, Green Label	5/-	2/9
Bass's Pale Ale	—	5/6
Worthington's Pale Ale	—	5/6
Guinness's Extra Stout	—	5/6
Lager (Graham's)	—	6/6
„ (Heineken's)..	—	8/-

18

CYDER

Henley's or Whiteway's Devonshire and Coates' Somerset.

In Cask 4½ galls. and upwards .. .. .. per gall. 2/-

	Per doz.
Imperial Quarts	10/-
Imperial Pints	6/-
Imperial Half-pints..	4/6
Champagne Cyder (Reputed Pints)	6/-
Champagne Cyder (Nips)	4/-

MINERAL WATERS
SPECIALITIES.

Brewed Ginger Beer. In Cask or Stone Bottles.
Specially brewed from a very old recipe, from Best Jamaica Ginger and Pure Cane Sugar.
Per Gallon (In Cask) 2/6
Per Dozen (In Bottles) 2/9

Dry Ginger Ale. A very high class and nice flavoured Dry Ginger. A good digestive per dozen 2/9

Vimto. A very favourite fruit tonic with Port flavour .. .. .. per dozen 2/9

Grape Fruit Squash. Made from the actual juice of the finest Grape Fruit .. per dozen 2/9

Cyder Snap (non-alcoholic) prepared from Devonshire Cyder .. .. per dozen 2/6

Quinine Tonic. Very pleasant and of medicinal value 2/6

continued overleaf

19

Pages from Wadworth's very extensive price list of the 1930s. The range was impressive and the list included no less that 21 different ports, 13 sherries, 19 liqueurs, 20 whiskies and a large choice of table wines and soft drinks.

and sometimes somebody would put some pennies in the fire on a shovel and get them red hot and then drop them into the crates. Then poor old Dick would come along, shake the crates and out would fall the hot penny and he'd pick it up and ...aarg! It was cruel but we did laugh.

Cecil Scratchley

Rivalry

I was an apprentice fitter on steam engines at W.E. Chivers during the war. The steam engine men considered themselves superior to the motor mechanics but in time, of course, it came about that the motor mechanics outnumbered the steam fitters and there was always rivalry between the foremen of each group. If the motor mechanics wanted something machining, for example, the fitters would always be too busy to do it, and so on.

Ralph Merrett

Getting the Orders

I eventually became head clerk for Wadworths and then went on the road after that, as a representative in March 1953 and I continued doing that until I retired in 1988. It was mostly private trade when I started and I used to

69

visit houses in all the villages around; Worton, Marston, Aldbourne, Marlborough and so on, covering about twenty houses in each village. There were six rep's at the time and the deliveries were done later by lorry. We were expected to get a minimum of thirty-three orders a day, every day. It was mainly bottled stuff, beer, flagons of cider, tins of crisps and bottles of orange squash. We sold a lot of sherry in those days and oatmeal stout too, which you don't see so much now. You'd try to build up your own rounds and get new customers all the time. I used to go down the garden to see them sometimes, if they weren't in the house. A man might be planting out his beans and I would kneel down with him and chat to him saying something like, 'I'm from Wadworths in Devizes, I expect you could do with a pint after hard work like this, we can deliver to your door!' I'd get new accounts like this and earn extra commission.

The office on the corner of the brewery, it's not used as an entrance any more, was used as the reception and the place where people came to pay their accounts. When someone came in to pay I would greet them with a, 'Good morning, sir', and then I'd say, 'Would you like a glass of beer, sir?' Then I'd pour them a glass of Amber Ale from a bottle, taking care to pour it out with a good head and that would go down really well. They used to come in and pay their bills then!

I'd get back at night at about half past six. Eventually when we got cars, and at first I got the old ones that had been clapped out by somebody else, you didn't keep it at home. I had to take it back to the brewery, park it in the garage and go home on my bike! My first one was an old Morris.

Cecil Scratchley

Some of the staff of the Bear Hotel photographed in the garden in about 1918.

CHAPTER 4

Carnivals, circuses and fairs

Devizes Pleasure Fair in about 1900.

The Pleasure Fairs

The pleasure fairs were wonderful things when I was a boy. I loved the carousels and still do. Coconut shies were very popular and there were lots of side-shows. I remember going to see the fat lady and being staggered at the size of her. One of the side-shows was a girl in a coffin wearing only a sparkly triangle somewhere over her middle! She was surrounded by a high parapet and all the lads of the town were leaning over to have a good look and many were staying there for as long as they could!

We enjoyed the swing boats and 'over boats' which went right over the top. There was also one called the American Aeroplane which went round and round tipping to each side. They were crammed with people, especially at night. In the early days before they used electric light naphtha flares were used which seemed very dangerous. Some rides had waterfalls at the side with coloured lights on them. The town on fair days was alive even before it was light.

Leonard Strong

Fairings

A traditional thing to buy was fairings. These could be bought at the fair but we made them at the bakery to sell from the shop. For weeks before fair days my brother and I were co-opted, in the afternoons, to help with the fairings. From morning to night people would be coming into the shop to buy them. Fairings were very crisp sweet, flat biscuits and we made them in large quanti-ties. They were on sale all the year round but most were sold during the fairs. We made them with butter, golden syrup and flour and flavoured with ginger. The syrup was boiled up with the butter and then the flour was mixed in and the ginger added. We had a great bath of the mixture in the outhouse where it was kept and the bakers came to collect bucketfuls to take into the bakery. It was rolled out into long soft pieces and then chopped up into little bits and baked in the oven on tins. They melted and boiled out into flat shapes. After they were baked they were cooled on the trays placed on the bakery floor. When they were cool they went crisp and could be moved. They were shovelled out and we would put them into great canisters to be stored. We had drawers full of ready weighed up fairings in pound and half pound bags to sell in the shop.

Leonard Strong

The Fairs

We never went to the fairs, it was one of our greatest sorrows that our parents believed they were terrible places. We had to stay away from them. We'd walk up to the Green and have a look and then go past and back home again. We were a very puritan family. We were not even allowed to go to the mayor and mayoress's soirée for children at Christmas although my father was on the council.

Lillian Hinxman

72

The Jennings' Gallopers on Devizes Green, *c.* 1910.

A production of *Snow White and the Seven Dwarfs* played in the castle grounds in about 1916. The event was organised by Mrs Oliver and included Phyllis Strong and a young Leonard Strong as one of the dwarfs.

Sheep and Horse Fairs

The small Green and part of the big Green were covered with hurdles for the sheep, which were brought through the town, down Monday Market Street and Sheep Street. An area of the Green was kept free of sheep, in the middle and at the back by the school, for the horses. The top Green, by Heathcote House, was usually covered with gipsies carts and vehicles. The horse fairs went on until after the war.

Chris Bush

Devizes' Fairs

Large numbers of livestock would arrive in town on fair days, cattle galore, bulls, horses and sheep. In those days many would arrive by train, there was a big stockyard down at the station. At the end of the day they would be driven back again to the station and it was nothing then to see cattle in the streets. On fair days you could always expect to see a bull escaped and at large, running through the town dragging its pole, drovers chasing it and trying to catch it whilst people scattered out of its path, hiding in doorways and shops. Cattle were sold at Candlemas Fair in Monday Market Street by the Castle Hotel. All the houses round there boarded up their windows because cattle could break the windows. At other times cattle were sold in the yard behind the Black Swan. Horses were sold outside the National Westminster Bank in the Market Place. During the school holidays lots of children used to congregate in the Market Place waiting for some animals to escape and then give chase to try and catch them! Animals would sometimes get into the shops. W.H. Smiths regularly had animals in it. In my accountancy days I worked in offices over the bank and animals often got into the building, chickens, pigs even a carthorse got into the space at the bottom of our stairs. There was a terrific noise and feathers everywhere!

Leonard Strong

The Whales

My father won me a lovely great china doll once on the hoop-la. I remember the 'Whales' ride at the Jennings Fairs. My father was friendly with Jim Jennings and we used to get free rides on them. There was a 'cake-walk' too that shook you about as you walked on it - shook the life out of you!

Joyce Rose

Hospital Carnival Week

This was always a week with lots of events. Mrs Oliver, who had the wool shop at the top of The Brittox, was a great organiser and socialite and was responsible for organising many of the carnival activities. She ran a terrific tombola from her shop and filled the window with things people had given as gifts. There would be coal from one person, logs from another, a dodger and cheese from a pub and all sorts of odd prizes. Strongs didn't give a prize because we were Baptists and didn't believe in any form of gambling. At the end of hospital week there was a full scale do in the Corn Exchange and Mrs Reed from the castle came to turn the handle on the tombola and take out the tickets.

On the Wednesday of the week there was usually a pageant in the castle grounds which was also usually organised by Mrs Oliver. On Carnival Day she headed the procession and was really the mainspring of the whole holiday and many local people took part in historical costumes. The town was decorated with fairy lights and candles and men

Elephants from a visiting circus drink from the fountain in the Market Place, late 1880s.

painted the glass panels on the gas lamps with different colours.

At the end of the First World War Mrs Oliver organised A production of *Snow White and the Seven Dwarfs* and I was a dwarf.

Leonard Strong

Mrs Oliver's Fund-raising

She organised a Whist Drive and a Tombola each year during the 1930s. I used to do the window display of prizes for the Whist Drives. We used White's window in Sidmouth Street. The Tombola prizes were not displayed there

A production of *Snow White and the Seven Dwarfs* at the Palace cinema in 1953. The dwarf on the right is Michael Oliver. It was 'a great success, three packed houses'.

were too many! She got prizes from everyone, when you won one you collected it probably from the person who donated it. We sold tickets in the street and everwhere for the Tombola - it raised thousands of pounds each year for the hospital.

Peggy Hancock

Devizes Circus

I remember on one occasion when we went to the circus there was a turn in which a group of performers were dressed as angels, in floating garments, they were hauled up to the top of the post and hanging by their teeth they went floating round and round the post. Another time I remember seeing bareback horse riders dressed as clowns riding round the ring, standing up, flinging off clothes as they went round until they appeared dressed in wonderful coloured

tights and costumes, looking more like princes than clowns. There were also elephants and lions and a whole menagerie of animals to go and see. There would always be a procession through the town to advertise it with the band playing on the top of one of the decorated vehicles. In those days everyone who had a shop lived above their premises and so when there was a procession of this kind everyone would be leaning out of their windows to watch. We would watch from our windows in The Brittox as people performed up and down the street. They had long poles with bags on the end so that they could reach the top windows to collect money. The elephants were taken to the drink at the Crammer. The Crammer at that time was almost always occupied by animals of some sort, horses and cattle especially.

Leonard Strong

CHAPTER 5

Shops and shopkeepers

Mr Scudamore with his daughter Violet outside the Singer Sewing Machine shop that he managed in the High Street, 1922.

Simpson's shop in the Market Place, *c. 1906.*

Family Shopping

As we had a business in town we always did our shopping in town too. We expected people to come to us so we never thought of going any where else. Groceries we would get from the International Stores in The Brittox and meat from the butchers in the High Street. We didn't need to buy much fruit because we grew most of that but I can remember using Barlow's at the far end of the Market Place and the market. Clothes we bought at various places, Beales, Madame Hilda's in Maryport Street and my mother would sometimes go to a Miss Bird's in Sidmouth Street. Shoes we got from Dodge's, and later, from Brewser's in The Brittox. A lot of your shopping went with where you went to church; chapel supported chapel and church supported church, on the whole.

Olive Chivers

Simpson's Grocery

The floor of the shop was sanded and Mr Simpson would emerge from a door to the left to greet you. There were shelves of groceries all around the shop. In the first week of December there would be a display of ingredients for the pudding and you knew Christmas was coming. I had a lovely feeling as I walked by to school and saw the currants and things and, all along the top of the window, crackers in boxes. He roasted coffe and this was the smell as you passed by. We only had coffee when we had people to supper. On Sundays we always had a cake from Simpsons, a plain cake with a sweet top.

Lillian Hinxman

No Sunday Trading

My father was born at 24, Sheep Street. My grandfather was born in Potterne and moved to Devizes, married a girl called Hughes and lived in a little cottage in Carmel's Court behind number 24, Sheep Street. My grandmother had a little grocery and sweet shop there and my grandfather was a gardener. They were great Baptist people and just about the time of the outbreak of the First War she got struck off the list! Someone came round to her back door on a Sunday morning wanting some soap and she sold it to her. The Baptists got to hear of this and she was 'struck off'. They didn't go there anymore, my father and the rest of us went to St Mary's.

Bill Underwood

Cheesecakes and Simnel Cake

Many of the specialities in a business such as ours originated from the need to use up 'stales'. Things like Banbury Cakes and Eccles Cakes, I think, had in the mixture stale cake. Our business specialised in sponge goods, very fine sponge goods, which were made into all sorts of things. One of the ingredients of the Devizes Cheesecake curd is sponge crumbs, so this was an outlet for using up the stale sponge.

Another speciality of the establishment was an original Simnel Cake. This cake that was made in our businesss for Mother's Day and in Lent, originated I think, from the story about Simon and Nellie; Simon liked things boiled and Nellie liked things baked and so they made a cake that was boiled and then baked. I remember it and it *was* actually boiled and then baked. My father used to sell it and he always used to say that he felt like apologising for it because he couldn't believe that they enjoyed it! It was a star-shaped cake, made with bun dough, it had saffron in it and a lot of fruit and peel. The whole mixture was shaped into a star and then boiled in a saucepan of water for a time and then taken out and baked. After it was baked

The Strong family in 1911. Joseph Strong, the baker, with his wife and children; Leonard (standing), Stewart, Phyllis and Jack the dog.

it was glazed and it was very hard! I remember my father saying, because he was so ashamed of it, that the way to eat it was to cut it into thin slices and soak it in Port wine! We also made lardie cakes, of course, and these were a favourite. No-one today makes them like they used to be made.

Leonard Strong

Devizes Barbers

Underwoods were in Sheep Street and there was Bert Barnes on the corner of Sheep Street, where Duck's first shop was later. There is a story

Bert Sanders' shop in High Street, c. 1922. Bert (right) sold the business to Bob Cook (left) in 1925.

about when Gilbert came for a shave there and couldn't wait long because his horse was too frisky. Bert told him to bring the horse inside while he had his shave - and he did. There was a Mr Young in New Park Street and in the Market Place was Williams's, upstairs over a tobacconists shop, just along from the Midland Bank. One of the hairdressers that worked there was Alec Bridges whose father had his own business next to the Rising Sun in Estcourt Street.

Bill Underwood

The Singer Shop

My father came from Bath to work for Singer Sewing Machines and run the sewing machine shop in the High Street. He was a baker really and had his own business in Bath before

coming to Devizes but, sadly, had lost it. I was born just after my parents arrived in Devizes and I was brought up mainly by our housekeeper because my mother was an invalid. I was never involved in running the shop and after leaving school I worked as a secretary.

Violet Scudamore

High Street Butcher

After the War in 1918 my father came back to Devizes and joined his brother in the business at 9, High Street. Later, in 1921, he bought the business and ran it himself. My father's assistant at that time was a man called Beadle, he would deliver the meat to the customers and also collect carcases from the slaughterhouse in the horse and cart. In 1924 Beadle left and Bob Cook started who was eventually to take

Price and Son's music shop in Handel House in the 1930s. Peggy Oliver (left) stands behind the counter with Walt Ellis (piano tuner) and Hilda Bond.

over the business himself and in whose family's hands it is still run today, although not in the same shop. The meat my father sold all came from a farm at All Cannings which, I think, was owned by Herbert Douse. Dad would walk around the fields selecting the cattle he would like and it was slaughtered on the farm and the carcases collected later.

Later on we had a Ford Type T van for the deliveries which doubled as a tourer for the weekends. It had inter-changeable bodies on the same chassis. It had three gears; high, low and reverse and gravity feed petrol. If you were going up a steep hill and the petrol was a bit low it would stop. When we went out at weekends we filled up when we saw a garage because they were few and far between. There was a choice of Pratts, R.O.P. or Ethyl.

Tom Sanders

The Music Shop

I went to work at Price's Music Shop in Handel House in 1926, straight from school, and stayed for fourteen years, until I got married. Selling records and music was what I did for most of the time but later on I took on the book-keeping and sending out the bills. We used to send out bills for tuning, five shillings a time or a pound for five times a year. The number of bad debts you got at that rate was terrific! I used to stick little labels on them saying, 'unless...', and I knew when I sent some of them out that it was going to be a dead loss and that I might just as well have torn them up straight away.

We had several full-time tuners, Walt Ellis was the head tuner who eventually went off to work on his own. Jim Gillett was another one of our tuners. We had a full-time polisher, Bill Smith, who French polished the pianos; he was a very good polisher and lived in

Price and Son's music shop in Handel House, 1930s. This group, photographed in the gallery where the pianos were displayed, includes, left to right: Bill Smith (french polisher), Peggy Oliver (later Hancock), Jim Gillett (piano tuner), Hilda Bond and Walt Ellis (piano tuner).

Bromham. Price and Sons was a big company, based in Bournemouth, Dennis Price used to come up every Thursday or so and everyone would be on their best behaviour! They had shops in Bournemouth, Boscombe, Amesbury and Yeovil. In those days everyone had a piano and we didn't have much competition in the town, there was only John Nott in the High Street, he did some tuning. We sold mostly pianos, the gallery was full of them and they were all carried there up the back stairs. We sold a lot of sheet music and the piano teachers came to us, Molly Brown [Trumper] was one and Mrs Bourne was a cello teacher who lived in Trafalgar Buildings. Sheet music cost sixpence a copy before the war and we sold more of that than recorded music although we did sell quite a lot of records, both classical and popular.

We used to get the gypsies, or didikois as we called them, in the shop when there was a fair on the Green. They used to come and ask to hear Irish music. They would bring their babies with them a sit and breastfeed them in the shop while they were listening. They didn't very often buy the music, just came in to listen and feed the babies!

It was my job to decorate the windows, I enjoyed that. I dressed a window once with a stuffed lion borrowed from Billy Dickenson the bookmaker and grandfather of Keith, now at the Bear. The lion had a record in its mouth and a sign saying, 'Music soothes the savage beast'.

Peggy Hancock

Underwood's the Hairdressers

Father opened up the shop in Sheep Street in November 1913 when he was sixteen. His mother had put up the money to rent it and on the first day he waited for a customer. He spotted a friend coming down the road towards the shop and thought he would have a joke on him. There was only a cold water tap and a bucket in the shop at that time and he filled a sponge with cold water and waited in the corner. As the door opened he threw the wet sponge at a stranger who had come up from the other side and entered ahead of his friend!

Father learnt his trade as an apprentice with Walt Knott in Sidmouth Street, you can still see his name up on the wall by his old shop today, 'W.A.Knott, Tobacconist'.

My brothers and I all worked in the shop from quite an early age. We would start as lather boys at twelve years of age, lathering up the men for shaves. Father would shave them as they were ready and then we sponged them off and took the money. The very first customer I lathered up was Gerry Ruddle, who was one of the leading firemen; he and Jack Webb were heroes of all the small lads in the town. It was tuppence for a shave and as I finished wiping him off he gave me the money and I said thank you very much and put it in my pocket. I told my dad that he was very kind and had given me tuppence and he said, 'That's not for you it's for the shave, put it in the till!' Lots of men came in for a shave every day but some only once a week. The old farm labourers came in on Thursdays or Saturdays. There was an old Irish labourer called Paddy who worked for Gilbert at Hartmoor and came in for a shave once a week and once every six months he had a haircut. He had it all shaved off right over, that was usually our job when we were boys since it didn't

A window display at Price's music shop in Handel House in the 1930s. Peggy Oliver won awards for windows like this one.

require any skill. Several people had this done.

My father worked long hours to keep our large family. He worked until eight at night but closed at six during the War. Before he opened up in the morning he went to the hospital and shaved all the patients, then he visited all the 'specials' who were shaved in their homes including Frank Chivers, the coal merchant, and Fred Chivers the builder. He didn't close for lunch but grabbed something to eat while the lather boys were getting the next customers ready. He opened for shaves on Sunday mornings too. He worked very hard.

Bill Underwood

A fashionably turned out pair! Ralph Merrett and Bill Underwood outside St Mary's church in about 1953.

Loyalty to One's Customers

We had four milkmen and three bakers because they all came to my father as customers for a haircut. I can't remember how many butchers we used, but each day my mother seemed to go to a different one and on some days to Alfie Robbins for faggots and peas, he had a little faggots and peas shop in New Park Street, but my father's downfall, I think, was that he had about thirty-six publicans as customers and he tried to drink with them all!

Bill Underwood

The Strong's Shops

The family of Hook had a bakery business in The Brittox at number 7 [now A.T. Mays and the kitchen shop] which in 1862, along with two other properties, was gutted by fire. The business was transferred to the little corner shop in Long Street, behind the Town Hall, opposite the Elm Tree. My grandfather, who originated in Upavon, opened, at this time, a bakery shop in The Little Brittox where Kirk's shop now is. They made a bakery in the cellar, under the shop, the only access to it was down a steep ladder. The millers, when they came with the flour, had to put the sacks on their backs and go down this ladder to the bakery underneath. It wouldn't be allowed, under any circumstances, today! The bakery, I believe, still exists. My grandfather, I suppose, was an opportunist, and he thought that as the big establishment in the big Brittox was gone, because of the fire, that he would start one there in The Little Brittox. He brought up his family there in the house above the shop. Hook's shop moved back into The Brittox in about 1865 and was restarted there by John Bowden and his daughters. They also used to do meals as well in what was called the Phoenix Restaurant, as it had risen from the ashes. It continued with John Bowden until he died then it was run by his daughters until 1892 when Mrs Bowden retired and my grandfather took it over. In 1903 my father, who had been working in Cardiff as an apprentice watchmaker to his brother, came back to Devizes and married. When my grandparents died my father took over the business. It was intended that I would

The Brittox in about 1900. On the left is Strong's bakers shop and the Phoenix Restaurant, then came Mrs Willis's toyshop 'with skipping ropes and hoops at the front', then Miss Chivers' and Miss Smith's fruit shop 'with homemade pickles and jams'. Next to this was a newsagent and tobacconists shop run by Mrs Taplin.

go into the business too, when I left school at sixteen, but this did not go down well at all. My father was not a good teacher and it only lasted about six months! I left and he found me a job in an accountant's office in Devizes in 1922. I eventually transferred to the London office and although I did not really want to work as an accountant I eventually started a correpondence course to take an accountancy exam. I studied in the kitchen of my digs for this exam and when I took it I failed in every subject! In 1932, when my father was getting on in years, I wrote to him and said that I would like to go into the business, I wouldn't want to go into the bakery but I would look after the business side and manage that. Against his better judgment he consented to let me do that! I came back and started trying to make some changes. My father paid me one pound a week from which he deducted insurance! This was barely a subsistence but was all the business could stand at the time. I lived at home and worked in this way for nine years.

The premises at 7 and 8 The Brittox were rented at eighty pounds a year from the Almshouses Trustees who announced out of the blue one day that the premises had been sold to a property

Advertisement for Strong's bakery and restaurant in 1931.

speculator and my father was given notice to leave. This happened in about 1938. We had always assumed that we were secure there for the rest of our lives but were now faced with the prospect of having to move. My father could find no suitable premises in Devizes to continue the business and began to look outside the town.

There was at this time a business in the town called C. Neate, upholsterers, antique dealers and undertakers who had a substantial business in Maryport Street, where Tesco now is. The business was run by Roland Neate, who was mayor during the First World War, his elder brother Edward who was the undertaker (and who used to rub his hands when a good funeral came along) and a third younger brother who was consumptive. The firm also had premises in the Market Place which they used as a depository for the antique furniture

and where they also kept coffin boards and made coffins. At about the time my father was seeking new premises, Roland Neate died and the Neate family decided, as Edward was getting on and the younger brother was not well, that they would give up the business. The shop in the Market Place was offered to my father. Although it was not ideal it had a lot of outbuildings at the back which could be converted into a bakery and it seemed to be a godsend. Although my father was not an adventurous sort of man and did not like the prospect of taking on such a proposition he decided to try to buy the building.

His own bank which was Barclays in The Brittox [now the Bon-Ton] would not advance him the two thousand pounds or so that was required but the Midland Bank, where my brother was employed, did. With the help of Raddons, the undertakers in Sidmouth

86

Street, and Ottoways, the plumbers, my father refitted the shop with a cafe restaurant upstairs, the shop downstairs and the bakery at the back. My father intended that we should live as a family over the shop but my mother said that she would not under any circumstances live there. She was a remarkable woman and had a very strong character and held strong views and she said she would leave my father rather than live in the Market Place! She had never enjoyed being close to the business and so it was decided that she should have what she had always wanted and that was to live away from the shop. A house was found in Bath Road and she then ceased to be involved in the business. This was very good for me because it was my opportunity to become more involved in the running of the business but it was also just at the beginning of the war and I had received my calling-up papers. My father could not see how he would manage and made an application for me to be 'reserved' on the grounds that I was needed to help him run a food business. His application was successful and I was kept from going into the services providing that I was a partner in the business, this I became and for the first time in my life I had two pennies to rub together. One of the first things I did with my new opportunity was to begin to develop the new premises. My cousin's husband was Alfred Chivers, then head of W.E. Chivers, and in 1940 I borrowed from him one hundred pounds with which I bought furniture and carpets. Within six months I had paid him back - the town was full of evacuees and there were many people who wanted an establishment such as ours. I could see the

Neate's furniture depository and shop in the Market Place in about 1906 which was bought by Joseph Strong in 1939 for his new shop and restaurant.

potential it had and was able now to make use of it to the full. The restaurant held forty-seven people at a time and during the War we often had it fully booked for two sittings a day. We had a food allowance, not coupons because they were not used for restaurant meals, and had to send in a return for the meals we had served. We were allowed an amount of meat, sugar and so on each week. We had a meat allowance of thirty shillings a week. The rest had to be found by contrivance of some kind! There was plenty of fish, Mr Batt the fishmonger used to serve me well. Dried egg was used to make omelettes. I had to develop a flair for coping with the shortages at that time.

After the War I converted a loft at the rear of the restaurant into another dining room. It was opened generally on

87

The restaurant at the rear of Strong's shop in the Market Place, converted from an old loft, probably soon after it was opened in the early 1950s.

Thursdays and Saturdays and we let it out for special functions. I used to do a ladies' dinner party in there for the Rotary Club every other month.

The business continued in my hands until 1973 when I retired and sold the shop and business.

Leonard Strong

Shopping for Clothes

I got a lovely pair of brown leather shoes for 7/6 from Stead Simpson in The Brittox and you could get a nice summer dress for 5/-, which was just as well because even though I worked at Wansboroughs as a good shorthand typist I only got £3 a week. This was in 1946.

Gwen Chivers

Oliver's Wool Shop

I used to keep a good stock of wool, enough to supply people, not like today when no-one keeps very much. I bought wool in hundredweights, my husband used to carry it all upstairs for me. The room above the shop was full of wool, all around the walls. It's the only way to do it, you don't want a bit here and a bit there, the colours wouldn't match for a start.

Next door, where the opticians is now, was Taplin's restaurant and bakery and at the back, up some steps, was the workshop where they printed the *Advertiser* and they had their office round the corner where the toyshop is now. There is a part of the building at the back, behind Rutters, which we used to keep chickens in during the war. We had a lot of eggs from them! At one time Devizes had five wool shops and

ASHWORTH,

Portrait & Commercial Photographer

(Day and Electric Studio),

8, MARYPORT STREET, DEVIZES.

GROUP PHOTOGRAPHY :

Groups taken anywhere at any time.

THE AMATEUR PHOTOGRAPHER

can get every want supplied at our Studio.

Advertisement for Ashworth, photographer in 1933.

now it has none but it has five travel agents! It's all changed, I wouldn't want to be in business now.

Peggy Hancock

Kemp's Outfitters

My father came from Kent to buy the shop in The Brittox from a Mr Evans in 1901 and the business stayed in the family's hands right up to 1996. My brother Roy took over from my father and then my nephew Robert followed him. Like most families who had shops in those days we lived above the shop, I was born there in 1909. It was very good to be able to watch what was going on from the upstairs windows! I can remember seeing prisoners of war being marched up The Brittox from the station to the barracks at Roundway during the First War. We watched the carnival processions and had a good view of everything. It was a such a pity, I think, when they closed The Brittox off.

Miss Kemp

Photographer

Our family photographer was Mr Ashworth in Maryport Street. He had a bushy beard and looked like George Arliss!

Jack Fell

The Baker and the Maids

We made all sorts of bread, it was a country bake and it was delicious.

Mr and Mrs Hiscock at the back of their house in Jeffrey's Court in the early 1950s.

Sunday off. Most of these girls came from the country and in those days the poorer families couldn't wait for their daughters to leave school so that they could go into service and be paid what was a ridiculously small sum of money. They lived-in, which was very convenient for their employers, but it was not very good for the girls. It is an extraordinary thing to recall now that in my family, from the beginning of the century to when I was about thirty years of age, no-one ever dreamt of getting a meal, clearing it away or washing it up because it was the duty of the maids to do so. We never thought of ever doing anything like that.

Leonard Strong

The Best Range of Beers, AWs, Wines and Spirits Around

Even in the thirties Wadworths had a very wide range of other drinks for sale besides their own products. We could provide home deliveries for them all and this explains why we had such a good home trade, that and because customers only had to pay after three weeks because that was how often we called. There was also the retail shop in St Johns Street, Giddings, which is still there. The original Giddings shop used to be where the Anglo Swiss was, and now the Town Hall Vaults off-licence is, and Wadworths bought the premises and they retain the original name to this day, although using the premises opposite. In the 1940s the shop was managed by Mr Payne with an assistant, Mr Clark, who was also known as

It kept very well and had a wonderful flavour. The bread dough was made up the day before and set to ferment during the night and when the bakers came in at about five o'clock it was ready for them to work on. It used to be the custom that the head baker came in on Sundays to start the dough going for Monday. Much later I learned from the baker that there were often high jinks between the maid and the baker on Sundays while the family were at chapel. We kept two maids at the time and they took it in turns to have a

'Molotov' on account of his little round, Russian style hat. We had a big range of AWs [aerated waters, soft drinks] which were made at the brewery in the buildings facing Northgate Street. All the buildings from the corner to the White Lion pub was AWs. Mr Woodward, the foreman, lived on the premises in a cottage. It was possible to buy soft drinks from this part too. I remember we used to bottle Vimto - a lovely drink that was!

Cecil Scratchley

Sheep Street People

Harry Hunt had a butchers shop on the left-hand side going towards Hare and Hounds Street. They had their own slaughter house. When the Prince of Wales pub closed, which used to be between Handel House and the Baptist church, sometime just before the War, he moved there. His eldest daughter, Melba, married Reg Turner who worked at Roundway Hospital and when he got called up in the War he went into the RAF and was eventually reported 'missing, presumed dead', in the Far East. After about a year she remarried but after the war Reg came back again.

George Darley lived up at Selby's Yard and was marvellous with animals, he wasn't a vet but he knew what to do if you had problems with an animal. 'Shuck' Edwards used to drive the dustcart. He came here from London, a real spiv of a chap when he arrived. There was 'Gypsy' Smith and his family, all girls, who lived in Carmel's Court. He and his wife smoked clay pipes and he

Alf Hobbs in the garden of 3, Carter's Place, Sheep Street on leave during the Second World War.

worked for Wilts County Council on the roads. He always had a lovely smell of tar about him when he came in for a haircut. There was Cox Smith, he was a chimney sweep and a very keen fisherman, I think he died while I was away in the army. Next door but one to him was Ben Merritt, he was a chimney sweep too and we had them both to sweep our chimneys but on alternate visits. With all the coal fires you had to have your chimney swept several times a year. There were three sweeps altogether in Sheep Street at one time.

There was a big family called Mays about half way down the street, some of them worked on the dustcart, and I remember seeing the children sitting in

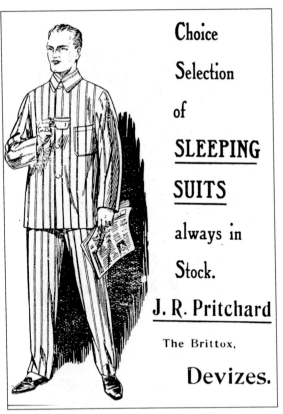

An advertisement for Pritchards in The Brittox in 1923.

a row on the pavement at dinnertime eating their bread and jam. There was a fish and chip shop run by Mrs Trout. Her best-known saying was, 'If you don't want the chips take the baby's bottom off the counter!'

Bill Underwood

Little Brittox

Pritchards was a high class mens' outfitters on the corner of The Brittox and Little Brittox, which later became Hepworths and is now a shoe repair shop. Pritchards had a window display in a small window in The Little Brittox,

at the end of their main window, where they advertised Burberry's weatherproof things. The display had a piece of the Burberry fabric stretched tight on a slope with drops of water falling onto it all the time and running off again to show how weatherproof it was. It was always something we would look at as we went through The Little Brittox. Next to this was Young's the hairdressers, where I used to go to have my hair cut. I paid tuppence to have it cut then, I pay four pounds and something now.

Leonard Strong

High Street Shops in the 1920s

On the corner with The Brittox was the International Stores then coming down the street was the hotel and restaurant that was burned, then there was a draper's shop owned by a man called Hathaway who had a big family, eight children I think. After that was Mr Hayward the photographer and Budd's furniture shop, run by Miss, Mr and Mrs Budd. Next to them was Hinxman's the coal merchants and a little court that ran up behind the buildings to two houses and some very nice gardens. We rented a garden there for a while. Next there was a little sweet shop run by Mrs Noyes who also made icecream - I could tell some stories about her! When I was about seven she used to get me to go along the street to Mr Williams for her 'medicine' in a medicine bottle. It was actually brandy and quite often by the afternoon she was blotto and incapable of running the shop so I used to help out behind the

The Scudamore sisters, Violet, Joyce and Margaret in the garden that the family rented from Hinxmans the coal merchants in High Street, *c.* 1933.

counter! After Mrs Noyes was another court and Springfords was up there. Then came the butchers shop run by Mr Sanders. We used to play there and in the garden. There was a room in their house called John Bunyan's room, I don't know whether he had ever stayed there or not but that was what it was called. Next to that was Nott's music shop and Mrs Nott's gown shop. There were some more houses at the back and and then another house on the street. Where the new pub [Four Seasons] is now was Miss Rutter's restaurant that sold home-made cakes and things. After Ward's house was, and still is, the Elm Tree pub. The pub was owned by Mr Bishop who had two sons with whom I used to play sometimes in the stable yard at the back. We used to watch an old man shoeing the horses there. It was lovely in the High Street in those days, we felt like a community, each family

knowing all the others and each one going to its own church or chapel on Sundays. Most people in the High Street were 'chapel' then.

On the other side of the street, starting again at the top on the corner, there was Clappens the outfitters. Then there was a house in which lived a man who worked for the customs and excise. Springfords came next, up a long path through a rather scruffy garden was a tin shed where they did their printing. It is hard to imagine this now because it was where the little chapel now stands. The chapel was built for the 'Bretheren' in the mid-thirties and is not as old as it looks. The next shop along the street was Griffins the ironmongers. The shop was very big and went back a long way. Like my family, Mr and Mrs Griffin went to the Methodist Church in Long Street.

Where the record shop is now, was a

think for Wadworths, because there was a loading bay there as well, where barrels and things were unloaded. They were both very large people and we used to think that they went very well with the brewery! I used to get on with them alright but I dont think they really liked children very much. We used to play whip-tops and I remember John Nott one day sent his whip-top through their window! Oh boy, did we run!

Across the other side of the Chequers there was a derelict house where the garden is today and next to it a house where the Harris's lived. Mr Harris was an ostler at the Bear Hotel. The big house which is now a bookshop and the Bernardo's shop was lived in by an old lady who kept a bath house. There were no baths in High Street so we all went to her for our baths! She had a series of about six baths. Finally, at the end was the Penny Bank. We sometimes played for hours running up and down those steps.

Violet Scudamore

Figgin's Grocers

My Saturday morning jobs were cleaning the brass, dusting the back room, polishing the lino and going to Figgin's in Estcourt Street for the shopping. It was a big grocers and we used to get all our groceries there. They had sawdust on the floor and biscuits on display all along the front of the counter. You could get a big bag of broken biscuits for 2d. We used to call Mr Figgins, 'Figgy Pudding'!

Gwen Chivers

Mr and Mrs Scudamore in High Street in 1936. Mr Scudamore ran the Singer shop opposite where he stands for the photograph. Behind them is the entrance to the court and garden belonging to Hinxmans the coal merchants.

saddlers run by a brother and sister, Miss and Mr Dalloway. Mr Dalloway sat on a bench stitching his saddles. She was very fond of animals and ran a sort of animal hospital always taking in stray cats and if we took anything to her she would pay us a penny for it. A penny was a lot of money when I was a girl. Then there was a stable-like building which I believe belonged to Wadworths although they didn't keep any horses in it. Next was our shop, Singer Sewing Machines, and then two houses, the second one of which was the biggest and is now the delicatessen. Mr and Mrs Payne lived in this house and worked, I

Figgins grocery shop in Estcourt Street in about 1910.

Buckland's Shoeshop

My father, Arthur Buckland, started a shoeshop in Maryport Street with his brother, Bill, in about 1913. He married my mother in 1918 and I was born in 1920. The original shop was only half the size of the present one, it was the left hand half as you face it and the other half, nearest to Chapel Corner, was a sweet shop owned by Sammy Smart. His wife used to run it but we called it Sammy Smart's sticky sweet shop. Sammy worked as the gardener for Mrs Bartholomew at Moorlands House on Hartmoor. It was a big house that used to stand on the corner of Hillworth Road and Hartmoor where the bungalows are now.

My father was a shoemender and maker. At the time it was about the only decent shoe shop in town, others were mainly cobblers. He made a lot of boots for farmers and he used to make all my shoes too. My uncle Bill didn't

marry and lived with us for a long time but my mother used to get fed up with him because he was a bit too fond of the bottle! I used to help in the shop when I was old enough. In the cellar we kept the machines for finishing the shoes after they had been repaired and I used to go down and do all the inking. The menders went all round the edges of the leather with a machine and chucked the shoes down to me to finish them. I inked them over with black or brown, which ever they were, heel-balled them and then finished them off on the polisher. When I got married my father made a home for us at the back of the shop where the workshop is now, on the Monday Market Street side. As our children arrived we began to get a bit cramped and eventually moved out to Waylands when the houses there were being built.

Joyce Rose

Arthur Buckland, who started the shoemaker's business in Maryport Street, photographed in *c.* 1916.

Restaurants

And then there was Strongs in the Market Place, that was a lovely shop. We used to have parties in the long room at the back. There was also a lovely restaurant further along where the wine shop is now, next to the bank, called the Borough Restaurant.

Violet Scudamore

John Chivers the Photographer

When we were small we had a nanny called Miss Hatton who came from Redhill. We worshipped her but couldn't pronounce her name so we called her 'Sattin'. I think she worshipped us too. She eventually married John Chivers the photographer. He had a wonderful business in Sidmouth Street. In his studio, in a recess by a little window near the door, he had a stereoscopic viewer full of slides taken with a special camera that took a pair of pictures at eye-distance apart so that they had a third dimension effect. It was a great thing with no end of slides in it: Devizes in the early days of the century, skating on ice on the canal, fairs on the green, circus processions going through the town, Drews Pond Lane, Big Lane and lots of others. Many of them were tinted, not sepia but orange and other colours. I would love to know what happened to it, it would be marvellous to find it again now.

It was in the days when everyone used to have studio portraits taken of themselves and give them as Christmas presents and families used to display their studio photographs on the drawing room table. John Chivers was always recognised as an outstanding photographer. He was, however, a bit of a crank and he eventually abandoned his wife and son and went to live in a caravan in Southbroom Park and became a religious revivalist. He had some means of printing and would produce pamphlets which he distributed to all the houses during the night. He called it an Itinerant Mission of Repentance. He eventually caught pneumonia, because he had no heating in his caravan, and died. Many of the old photographs of Devizes were taken by him.

We often used to stay with the Chivers family as children. When my younger brother and sister were born my brother and I were farmed out for a while and had the choice of staying with a straight-laced aunt who lived in Devizes or with the Chivers, who we loved. One of us was supposed to go to each house but we both preferred to go to the home of our old nanny so we usually ended up going to both and changing over half way through!

Leonard Strong

Hot Cross Buns

I bewail the fact that it isn't possible to find a good hot cross bun anywhere nowadays. We used to make delicious ones! We would be making them all through the night before Good Friday to have enough in the morning, all stacked and put ready to sell. Boys of the town would buy them from us and put them in baskets and call them round the town, 'One a penny, two a penny, all hot!' As soon as it was light on Good Friday this was a familiar sound. You couldn't get anything for one a penny, two a penny now.

Leonard Strong

Sweets

There were a lot of sweet shops in the town when I was a child and on market days you could watch sweets being made. There was a stall that made peppermint sweets from a huge piece which was pulled and stretched on a hook until it was the right size and shape.

Violet Scudamore

Maryport Street Shops

Chapel Corner was always a clothes shop, ladies' and childrens' things,

Miss 'Cissie' Hatton who was nanny to the Strong family's children and who subsequently married John Chivers the photographer, *c.* 1918.

when I was small, Mr and Mrs Naylor ran it in the early 1920s then Robinsons took it over and then a Mr Holland. The shop occupied more space than that shop does nowadays, coming right round into Maryport Street to number 15, next to Smart's sweetshop. Then there was us, Buckland's shoeshop, then next to that was an electrical place, James's from Trowbridge. The manager Mr Moore took it over and was joined by Fred Bush. The next shop was Dee's grocers and also a china shop, Gibbons, they shared a front door but there was a separate door to the china shop as you

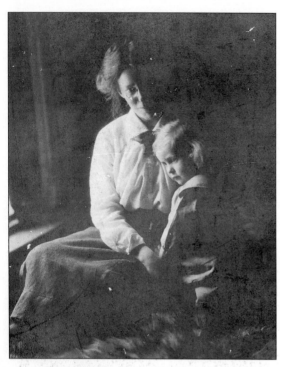

This unusual photograph was taken by John Chivers and printed with an orange tint to give a 'fireside' effect. It shows his future wife, Miss Hatton with Verna Strong . Before her marriage she worked as a 'governess' with the Strong children. This is one of many examples of John Chivers' experiments with photographic techniques.

went inside. There was another ladies' clothes shop after that, called Madame Hilda's, which was run by Mrs Plank. The next shop belonged to the Bacon Factory and this was followed by Mr Ashworth, the photographer. It was the thing, when I was young, to keep having your photograph taken, we used to go to him once a year and then to Mr Edmonds in Sidmouth Street the next. When you had a shop you had to share out your custom to others who used you. Just as when we went to buy groceries, we'd use Dee's one week and Lewis's the next because they both used to bring

their shoes in for repair. Next to Ashworth's studio was Mrs Harland's Dairy followed by a butcher's shop. The Oddfellow's Hall came next [now Halifax Building Society], which was used as a men's club downstairs and upstairs as a room for dances and music hall shows. In the 1920s there was a music hall every week which was very popular. We used to go to them all. Usually travelling companies put on the shows and if they stayed for more than a few days their children came to my school in Southbroom for a few days. The next shop was Lewis's grocers, a big double-fronted shop, now divided into two. Our weekly shopping list always had at the top, four pounds of sugar, for only four of us! My mother bought our fruit and tea on Saturday night from Mrs Smart, next door, rather than from the grocers. We had Salmon's Tea, which was fourpence a quarter, and saved the coupons. I've still got a nice vase that we got from these coupons. Then came May's furniture shop and finally, Johnson's the jewellers on the corner of Monday Market Street.

Joyce Rose

Devizes Businesses before the Great War

My uncle Ebenezer Strong had a jeweller's shop which was in the Market Place, next to Willis's the carriage works and garage, where the Co-op shop used to be, on the corner of Snuff Street. It was called New Street then. The garage went behind and along New Street. There were only about half a dozen people in the town with cars at that time. We used to collect motor numbers and try to find a number one first and then go up! The jewellery shop was eventually sold to Mr Leon Burn who was a well-known local worthy. In due course he moved from there to a shop next to Lloyds Bank.

Mr Willis bought the next-door property to his business and eventually converted it into a coach house and lived there with his family. As children we often used to visit them for tea and go up into the tower he built behind the house and look out over the Market Place. The house was called Tower House and the tower is visible in many old photographs of the Market Place. There is a similar tower on Melbourne House which was at that time owned by the Woodward family.

The Woodward family were printers and stationers who had before this time owned the shop on the corner of Wine Street. When Boots acquired the site for their new shop in 1912, it was later known as 'Boots Corner', the Woodward's business moved to Station Road where the Salvation Army now have a place. Several new buildings arrived in 1912; the Midland Bank was built where a provisions shop had been and further down the Market Place, several shops were demolished and the Picture Palace, or Electric Palace, was opened.

Opposite my father's shop in The Brittox was Walter Hill's chemists shop run by the redoutable Mrs Hill and where my mother had an account. She was a pleasant lady but you had to mind your Ps and Qs with her! Soon after the new Boots shop opened my mother went out one day and met Mrs Hill who

John Chivers the photographer in his own studio in Sidmouth Street c. 1900.

stopped her and said, 'Mrs Strong, I saw you coming out of Boots the other day, I don't know what you bought there but I hope it poisons you!' The building of the Boots' shop was a wonder to people at the time. Such a pretentious building where Woodwaards shop used to be! It was a beautiful shop with fancy goods upstairs and a lending library. The flag pole on the top flew a flag on all special occasions.

Next to the Boots' shop was Parsons, high class and military tailors. They were very superior tailors and people came from all over the country to have suits made there. Many ladies in the town worked there in the sewing workrooms. When later I worked in the

Wine Street and The Brittox soon after the opening of Boots in 1912.

Parsons and Son, a high class tailoring shop in St Johns Street, next to Boots' corner shop.

accountant's office just across the street, who did Parson's accountants, I was fascinated to look through their account books and see where all their customers came from. At that time they charged seven guineas for a suit and eight for a 'special'. Charlie Parsons, who ran the business, married the daughter of R.P. Mullings who started the building of The Breach. He built all the houses on the left side of the road.

Leonard Strong

Frankie Baker

There are many stories that people will tell you about a patient from Rounday Hospital called Frankie Baker. He was always to be seen around town and everyone knew him and liked him. He used to pinch milk bottles from doorsteps, drink the cream off the top, add two tea bags and some sugar then shake it up and drink the rest. He came into our shop nearly every day and we accepted him for what he was. One day I was cutting someone's hair and it was taking a long time because the customer was a great talker and I became aware of how impatient my next customer was getting, waiting for the next turn. I had almost finished when who should come in but Frankie. He came up to me (he used to talk mainly gibberrish) and said, 'I want a tube of toothpaste, a brush to go with it, a comb and a packet of razor blades'. 'Alright', I said, 'sit down and I'll sort you out in a minute', I knew he didn't really want anything. As I finished cutting the hair I could see him in

Roundway Hospital nurses displaying their new uniforms at about the time that these were introduced in the mid 1930s. They are Margaret and Joyce Scudamore.

the mirror recounting to himself these items, first on his fingers, and then after removing his dentures, on his teeth! I could also see the impatient customer looking at him in alarm so I quickly finished and just as he stepped from the chair, Frankie, who had just got through reciting his list of 'requirements' again, added, '... and a haircut to go with it' and jumped into the chair! Luckily I managed to usher him out of the shop with the request that 'he should come back later' and so I was able to continue with the next customer before he finally walked out!

He was so well liked that when he died, instead of the modest service and quiet burial usually held for patients at the hospital, his was a very well-attended affair with many people from the town turning up. Not having expected such a turnout the curate had to quickly find an organist. Ron Newman, who worked at the hospital, was organist for the hospital and he was found and the event became a much more suitable memorial service for him.

Bill Underwood

Miss Hampton's Dairy

Miss Hampton had a shop and dairy in Long Street, almost opposite the Elm Tree. It was run meticulously by Miss Hampton who was a well-corseted, imposing person with a big bust. She always dressed very neatly in a shirt blouse and a straw hat. She was an imposing woman and controlled the dairy with an iron hand. She organised, with great efficiency, the errand boys who delivered the milk and all the other activities of the business. She had an assistant who was called 'Cookie' and who helped manage the dairy. I remember the noise and clatter in the yard at the end of the day when the churns were being washed. We were sent down to get cream when it was being separated in the yard. It was the only place where cream could be bought. In the little shop Miss Hampton sold butter, cream and honey. The place was so well kept, it was so spotlessly clean and smelled lovely. We were told that the only time she lost her composure was when one of the milk boys let off a stink bomb in the dairy and she was heard to swear!

Leonard Strong

Jimmy Oram

We had in our family some Irish cousins, the Orams, and during a time of hardship their youngest son Jimmy, who was fifteen, came over from Ireland to work as the office boy in our coal merchant's depot in the High Street. He remained in Devizes when we left for Salisbury and became the boss of the firm and eventually mayor of Devizes. He was very popular and he never lost his Irish accent - everyone loved Jimmy Oram. He married Ida Talbot, the daughter of the drapers at the top of The Brittox and they lived at Belle Vue off the end of Northgate Street. Her mother, a widow, was an elegant lady who went to chapel in a black bonnet and mantle. I felt like I was with royalty when she came around. She had three daughters, one of them married one of the Strattons in Melksham, another a bank clerk (a step up) and the other married my cousin Jim. The Talbots also had a son who was most superior and would snub people he didn't want to talk to, even sometimes members of his own family! He always snubbed us.

Lillian Hinxman

Fire in the High Street

A big fire occured in the High Street where Springford and Rose's shop now is in about 1925. The building used to be a commercial hotel. Most of the businesses in Devizes, like elsewhere, were supplied by big firms who sent travellers round. Being a commercial traveller was a way of life in those days and because all big firms sold their goods in this way it was necessary to have commercial hotels to accommodate them. They were modest hotels which were found in all towns. This one was called Walkers when I first remember it. They used to dress their window with dishes of eggs and aspidistras in pots. As children we were always intrigued because at the back of the windows there were some low mirrors and we delighted to point out to visitors that if you got down and looked in them you could see that the aspidistra pots were really chamber pots with the handles broken off!

After the Walkers left the business it was taken over by a Mrs Haggard who was a district nurse and who lived there with her young son. From this time it always had a doubtful reputation and was regarded askance because she would accept any 'couples' who went in there. Its reputation was very low. One Whit Monday, when we still lived in The Brittox, we awoke in the night to see sheets of flame going up into the sky from a building in the High Street. It was Nurse Haggard's on fire! Everyone got up to go and watch as the fire brigade arrived. As the building burned the front wall fell out into the High Street. It was regarded as a first class fire, everyone enjoying it to the full! As the fire spread to the back it consumed part of Kemp's shop in The Brittox too and insurance money that followed allowed that business to rebuild and expand following the fire.

Leonard Strong

Mr and Mrs Horace Edmonds, *c.* 1948, behind the photographic studio in Sidmouth Street which he took over from John Chivers in 1925 when his business in High Street was destroyed by fire.

I don't remember very much of the fire that destroyed our house in the High Street and my father's photographic business because I was only four when it happened but I know something of it from my family's accounts of it. It was in 1925 and the fire started in Nurse Haggard's Temperance hotel next to us. My parents awoke to hear screams coming from next door and let Nurse Haggard's family into our house through a glass flat roof in the hotel. They were cut from the glass. I was picked up in a blanket from my cot and taken down the street to Sanders, the butchers, were we stayed for the night. I was laid on a couch and can recall hearing someone say that the fire was spreading fast and we may have to move on again soon. We stayed at the Lamb Inn for a few weeks after that and then Rendells made a house available for us in Long Street, until we could find somewhere to live. A town fund was set up to collect money for the families who had lost their homes in the fire and over £200 was raised. The burnt buildings were left as they were for a long time after the the fire and I can remember the smell of the charred remains as we walked past them. John Chivers, the photographer, is reputed to have said, of the fire, that it was an act of God to reduce the competition for his own business! He was at this time behaving in an eccentric way and soon afterwards gave up his business and moved into a caravan to conduct a sort of religious campaign. Ironically, my father took over his business in Sidmouth Street and continued to operate there for the rest of his career.

Barbara Wickett

I remember the fire that destroyed the restaurant and boarding house at the end of the Street run by Nurse Haggard. She had a reputation! It was not too long after the War, probably about 1925, and the place had a lot of soldiers staying there. The fire affected the rear of Kemp's shop, a garage, Edmond's photographers and a drapers as well. I was only very small at the time but I can recall seeing a lovely collie dog that was overcome by the smoke, lying on the pavement outside. The lady who ran the hotel before her, Mrs Walker, was a very distinguished lady. She came to see my mother once and she was dressed all in black and had a cane with a silver top. Nurse Haggard was supposed to have come for my birth but she came so late I was born before she arrived! Dr George, though, did arrive in time.

Violet Scudamore

Simpson's in the Market Place

There was a lovely smell of roasting coffee as you passed by Simpsons. My mother used to go there for her Christmas shopping, and buy the luxury things for her store cupboard. She would buy bunches of muscatel raisins which were put out with almonds at Christmas time and one year she caused my brother, who was with her in Simpsons, much embarrassment because it was always her custom to insist that they should open a fresh box of raisins so that she could have the first pick from the bunches in it! She also bought small children's oranges to save in her cupboard for Christmas.

Leonard Strong

The Fish Stall

On market days there were lots of animals for sale in the Market Place and most of the food stalls were in the Shambles. There was always a fish stall outside the Shambles at the back entrance. It was run by two brothers called Davis from Bradford on Avon. They didn't have a proper stall, the goods were all laid out on the ground and up on the wall. They were there every Thursday so we had fish for tea

Violet and Joyce Scudamore pose near their father's sewing machine shop in High Street in about 1938. The building behind them is an old stable, which was later converted into a shop and is now used by Devizes Lights.

every week. There were no Saturday markets in those days.

Joyce Rose

The Bowsher Sisters

Bowsher's Ironmongers Shop in the Market Place, was situated between Drew's seed, corn and hay merchants, where the present fish and chip shop is, and the Pelican Inn. Three Bowsher daughters ran the business. They were highly respected citizens in the town. Penny Bowsher ran the business side,

105

Market day in the early 1920s.

she was the 'brains' of the business. Being a woman she knew all the gadgets and things that woman would like in the kitchen better than a man. She knew every nut, screw and little item in the shop. She welcomed people with great gusto and affability and knew all her customers well. 'Yes, yes, yes,' I recall her saying, repeatedly, when serving people. Her younger sister Maud was a singer with an unusual and individual type of contralto voice. She was always called upon to sing at concerts in the Corn Exchange and elsewhere. The youngest sister was Kitty who ran the domestic affairs at home. They lived together all their lives until old-age overtook them. There was once a spectacular fire at their shop.

Leonard Strong

Coal Merchant's Shave

Mr Richards the coal merchant in the Nursery used to go for his shave at Underwoods in Sheep Street. He would stop off on his rounds and leave the horse and cart in the street. After he'd had his shave and haircut he'd come out with a clean face that didn't match the rest of him, so he would go up to his cart, rub his hands over the coal sacks and transfer some of the coal dust back onto his face so that it didn't look odd!

Ralph Merrett

Pork Butchers

The bacon factory in Bath Road had a shop in Maryport Street that sold all sorts of pork insides; chitterlings, pig's feet, bacon and pork.

Peggy Hancock

Advertisement for Hinxmans, 1956.

Sloper's Shop

Sloper's shop in The Brittox was run mainly by Tom Sloper who was a very clever man and an inventor. He had a workshop in Southgate, near the railway bridge, which is still standing. He invented some original tyres for aeroplanes in their early days. The tyres had a metal ring in the rubber and were called, I think, Palmer tyres. He was almost a recluse. In the shop there was a saloon upstairs for the ladies where the showroom was attended by assistants who used to sweep about all day in dresses with long trains. It was a very high class shop in those days.

The family of Slopers were Plymouth Brethren but Tom Sloper, who was a bachelor and lived with his sister, used to attend the Baptist chapel in Maryport Street.

Leonard Strong

Little Brittox Shop

When my grandfather moved his business to The Brittox he left the small shop in the hands of his eldest son, Tom Strong. He was quite a character but had little interest in baking. He left the running of the shop to his wife and worked instead as the senior assistant and managed the tailoring in a menswear shop run by his brother-in-law on the corner of the High Street and Wine Street, where The Gorge used to be. He was quite a wag in his way and enjoyed his social life! He used to sing at concerts and enjoyed such songs as, 'I do like an egg for my tea' and, 'Beer, beer glorious beer, fill yourselves right up to here!' My parents used to look upon this a little askance because we were chapel people. The shop in The Little Brittox was sold when Aunt Emily died in about 1935 and it was taken over by the Card family who ran a coach company and now run the oil supply business in the London Road.

Leonard Strong

The Brittox in the 1930s.

Manor Cottage in Estcourt Street, close to the corner with Estcourt Crescent, *c.* 1908. Florence Chivers stands at the door with her children, Laurie and Ethel.

CHAPTER 6
Wartime

Dylis Fell (centre) working for the Land Army at a farm near Ramsbury just after the war.

Butcher, Albert Sanders in the uniform of the Royal Flying Corps with his wife, Blanche and daughters Kathleen (left) and Dorothy. The photograph was taken in Mr Edmonds' studio in High Street in 1916.

The Cheese Hall Control Room

I did voluntary work at the beginning of the war in the control room in the Cheese Hall. It was a telephone control centre to warn the town of raids and other hazards. People manned the telephone in shifts and there was a policeman on duty and messenger boys. We were lucky in Devizes that not very much happened. We saw glimpses of the war; soldiers coming back from Dunkirk marched from the railway station to the barracks. What a sight they were, clothes in rags, very dirty and some being helped along by others. Later in the war German prisoners of war were also taken throught the town to prison

camps near Hopton Barracks.

Barbara Wickett

Chivers' Fire Brigade

During the war W.E. Chivers had their own fire brigades which were a bit like Dad's Army. There was one at Estcourt Street and another at the saw mills down Nursteed Road. It was meant to be a back-up to the ordinary one, which was nearby in Estcourt Street, or for fires at Chivers if they occurred. I was an apprentice fitter in Estcourt Street at the time. A man called Len Devin was the one who put us through our drill because he belonged to the regular brigade. We used to practice on Sunday mornings in the field next to the saw-mills. He would call out, 'Left turn' or, 'Right turn' and we were so bad that you would often end up with someone facing you, someone who didn't know their right from their left! The firemen were snobby, they wouldn't call the boys amongst them, that was me and Donald Sainsbury, firemen, we had to be 'firemen probationers'. We also had training exercises at night with the town fire brigade but such was the rivalry between us that the professionals didn't call us out until they had arrived at the scene and got 'water on' as it was called.

Ralph Merrett

Outbreak of War

When the War broke out the Wiltshire Yeomanry dug trenches on the Green outside the Drill Hall.

Devizes Firemen during the Second World War . At the back on the left is Don May, and third from the right is Jerry Ruddle. In the front row on the left is Jack Webb, in the middle is Fred Chivers and on the right is Percy Wells.

The Yeomanry had a big recruiting campaign in 1938 and it was said that if you belonged to them you could not get called up for the militia later if war started. They were billeted at the start of the War in the old school rooms in Sheep Street which had been empty for some time, before they went to war. All through the war there were soldiers staying there. There was a group of Service Corps there for a time who went to Africa and we heard later that they had all either been killed or captured in Tobruk. We also went to the old school to have our gas masks fitted. David my baby brother, had one of those big things that went right over him, we used to call it an 'iron lung', and my little sister Mary had a coloured 'Mickey Mouse' one.

Bill Underwood

British Rola

During the War British Rola came down to Devizes and set up in Pans Lane. They had been evacuated from Thames Ditton and were manufacturers of loudspeakers. I got a job there in the office doing wages and costings. I had to do a break down of costs for all the jobs and calculate the wages to be paid out, all from job sheets. It all had to be done manually using only an adding machine. You had to have brains to work in an office in those days! They had a sub-factory in Bridewell Street where there was some 'hush-hush' work going on developing torpedo tails. I had to take the wages round to Bridewell Street each week and pay them out as well. We didn't talk about the work they were doing there but I had to keep their worksheets each week. I'm not sure but I don't think they produced anything that was

Hinchley 1949 Ltd for a while and we continued by making just transformers instead of all the parts of loudspeakers.

Barbara Wickett

Land Army

I was very fond of the cows but I didn't always like the farmers! Once I was trained I got sent all over the county. We often lived very well, in fact, off the fat of the land at some farms despite the rationing. There was a farm I was sent to at Sutton Veny where the farmer was a real poacher. We had pheasant cooked in cream at Christmas and I had to skin and clean two deer during my time there, although I was only there for three months! We always had cream on our porridge. There was another girl there with me but he didn't like us going out at night - you can't just work on a farm and not have any relaxation. We decided to join the local young farmers' club but he didn't approve of that. We told him where we were going, the meeting was going to be held in a room over the Bell Hotel in Warminster. The next morning he wouldn't speak to either of us girls and he turned to the housekeeper and said, 'I wonder if those drunks got home safe last night'. We probably hadn't had anything to drink at all, or perhaps just a little something to warm us up, for it was a frosty night, and we had gone in our uniforms. The next time we went there was a dance afterwards and we decided to stay for that as well. When we came back, on our bikes, we worried about whether he would be waiting up for us. We took our shoes off and carried

Joyce and Violet Scudamore by the Penny Bank in High Street c. 1943. Violet is in WAAF uniform.

ever used. Those of us brought up in Devizes were quick to notice the different ways and manners of the London staff who came with the firm to run the factory.

Although I had been deferred from war service to work in the factory I eventually joined the WRNS and stayed with them until 1946. When I came back to Devizes I was sent for by both my previous employers and offered my old pre-war jobs back. I decided to go back to Rolas. I met my husband there and we got married in 1949, which was also the year that Rola went bankrupt. Hinchleys took over the company and I stayed with them. It was known as

Dylis Fell of Brickley Lane working in the Land Army just after the war on a farm near Ramsbury which had been converted from an army camp. The calves are feeding from old ammunition boxes.

the bikes, tiptoing up to the farmhouse and under his window but luckily he didn't wake up. There were three dogs in the house and none of them barked either! After this I told the Land Army that I wanted to move because he was getting on my nerves and so I went to a Land Army hostel and went out on relief milking for a while.

Dilys Fell

Haircuts for the GIs

We used to charge one shilling for a haircut during the War. One day a Jeep pulled up outside the shop and an American officer came in and asked us what we charged for a haircut. We told him and he said, 'We'll pay you one and three for a haircut if you'll send your two lads up to the camp and cut the soldiers' hair. They were the Fourth Armoured Division and my brother and I went and cut their hair. I was only about fourteen at the time. We were amazed to hear the swearing of these soldiers! My father never swore and it was quite an eye opener for us. The soldiers were very generous and gave us American money and other things.

Bill Underwood

War Work

During the war I worked in Chivers' workshops making ammunition boxes, torpedo cases and field telegraph poles. Some people employed in the work were evacuees from London and the rest were from Devizes and the vil-

A group of wartime workers employed at W.E. Chivers' workshops building ammunition boxes photographed at Mr Edmonds studio in Sidmouth Street in *c*. 1942. Joyce Rose is on the extreme left of the middle row.

lages. I was there for about two years and it was the first proper job I'd had. I didn't really mind the work. My first daughter was about eighteen months old at the time. In about 1943 a group of us went to Mr Edmonds the photographer in Sidmouth Street to have our photograph taken in his studio, in our working clothes and straight from a shift.

Joyce Rose

Fuel Supplies

The railway station was used by the military a lot and troops on their way to the Plain would often go through the town after arriving at Devizes station. During the First World War the first Handley Page bombers flew from Netheravon airfield on the Plain and the whole supply of petrol for the planes came through Devizes station and was delivered to them by lorries in two gallon cans. The bombers used to go out about three times a week. My family were aware of this because we knew the supply sergeant from Netheravon.

Leonard Strong

Troops on the Plain

During the First World War there were many soldiers on the Plain. We saw a lot of them in Devizes and got to know some of them. The conditions for them on the Plain were often very bad and some died of pneumonia without ever seeing the war. We invited

'Phone 153. 'Phone 153.

G. HOWLEY,

Motor Cycle and Cycle Depot,

Estcourt Street, DEVIZES.

Agent for Norton, A.J.S., P. & M., Velocette, Matchless, New Hudson, etc., etc.

Any Make of Car, Motor Cycle, or Cycle Supplied. Cash or Deferred Payments.

Open and Closed CARS FOR HIRE at any hour, day or night.

OXY-ACETYLENE WELDING A SPECIALITY.

Exchanges made in Cars and Motor Cycles.

Advertisement for Howley's in 1932.

some of them into our house for baths because they got so cold and wet at the camps. One day some soldiers at the house were entertaining us with songs when there was a knock at the door and it was some of their colleagues who had lost them but stopped when they heard the sound of a familiar voice coming from our house!

Miss Kemp

War Photographs

During the First World War John Chivers was in terrific demand taking photographs of the Canadian Expeditionary Force on Salisbury Plain. He used to hire Howley's car, an old-fashioned Ford car, from their shop in Sidmouth Street, the only place in Devizes where you could hire one, and go out onto the Plain and photograph the soldiers. My brother and I sometimes went with him on these trips in the car. When it rained the windscreen, which had no wipers, had to be opened at the top to make a space to see through.

Leonard Strong

A Close Shave

In the early days of the Second War, the town was full of Irish labourers who came to build the army camp at Le Marchant and on one Saturday afternoon, I remember, the Green was absolutely full of these men lying on the grass after drinking at dinnertime. There had recently been some trouble in, I

Devizes Home Guard photographed by Mr Edmonds outside the T.A. Centre behind the Green.

think, Coventry where the IRA had bombed some place and a man had been hanged for it, so people were still nervous about it. In the afternoon an Irishman came into the shop and asked if he could leave his bags there while he looked for lodgings in the town. My father agreed and he went off. Later someone noticed that there was a ticking coming from one of the bags! There was much debate about what to do - should they evacuate the shop, throw the bags out or have a look in them. One man decided to look and found a number of alarm clocks in it!

Bill Underwood

Evacuees

Like most families we had some evacuees at our house. Two little girls arrived on the day before war broke out and as we only had two bedrooms they shared my bedroom with me. They were from Nazareth House which was run by nuns in London. One of the girls proved to be a bit of a problem for my mother, she was very difficult to please and tended to upset the younger one and she was moved on somewhere else by the nuns supervising them. The other girl stayed with us for much longer and was quite settled with us when one day she came home from school and said she was being moved on to a children's home on the following day. No-one had any say in her move and she wasn't even allowed to take the clothes with her that my mother had made for her. I felt so cross about the way she was being treated I went down to the Catholic church and complained to the father about it. I was only nineteen at the time but, of course, it didn't do any good.

Barabara Wickett

V.E. Day celebrations at the Liberal Club in St Johns Court.

The Gas Clock

During the War we had a lot of Americans in town and one day when Jim Jennings (he was the mayor at one time, owner of the fairground rides and noted for colourful language!) was in the shop waiting for a haircut and there were some American soldiers waiting as well. They were going on about how quaint this little town was and how everthing was bigger in America until Jim Jennings couldn't stand it any longer. 'Let me tell you something', he said, 'this town has the only gas clock in Europe'. He pointed to the clock on the wall of the shop which was mounted over the end of an old gas pipe that used to connect up with a gas mantle before we had the electricity fitted. The clock had the name of the maker on the front, Cole of Devizes, and he said, 'See this clock, it works on gas and was made in this town, I'll bet there is nothing like that in America'. I don't know whether they believed him or not but it put them in their place and they were quiet after that!

Bill Underwood

Sharing the Bath Water.

My father used to share Lord Roundway's bath water! During the Second War they were both in Palestine and Lord Roundway was the Brigade Commander. He knew that George Underwood the hairdresser from Devizes was there and when he wanted a haircut he would send up the line for him to come to brigade headquarters and give him one. Lord Roundway in return would offer him the chance of a bath but he had to wait until Lord Roundway had finished with the water first.

Bill Underwood

MENU   7. 9. 47.

Luncheon

Kidney Soup.

Steamed Cod – Parsley Sauce
or
Roast Beef – Yorkshire Pudding

New Potatoes
Carrots or Cabbage

Stewed Apples – Semolina Sauce
or
Stewed Damsons – Semolina Sauce
or
Semolina Pudding

Bread may only be served in place of soup or sweet

BEAR HOTEL
DEVIZES

A hand-written menu card from the Bear Hotel for 7 September 1947. The luncheon menu shows all the signs of post-war austerity and food rationing.

Silent Night

At Christmas 1943 in Sheep Street, one night, all the American troops were in town and the place looked like the Wild West; army vehicles parked all along and soldiers shouting and swearing, singing and fighting. I was in bed trying to get to sleep when I heard Miss Bayley's voice. 'Would you mind being quiet', she said, 'my mother's dying'. Suddenly it all went quiet and then someone started singing *Silent Night* and everyone gradually joined in. It was beautiful.

Bill Underwood

Postwar Land Army

Just after the War I was sent to Ramsbury where they were converting an old army camp into a farm. It was staffed by displaced persons and everything from the camp was being re-used. The Nissen huts had been stripped of wood which was used to build calf pens and the big calves used to eat out of ammunition boxes and my cow shed had been the latrines for the troops. There was a place we used to call the art gallery where an American soldier, just before D-Day, had decorated what had been their canteen with crayons. On the walls there was a life-size drawing of an American soldier lying down resting his head on his helmet. All around him were pictures of what he was dreaming of, beautiful girls and things. We used to roll the oats in there for the cows.

Sometime after this I was sent on relief milking to Oswald Moseley's farm near Aldbourne. It was the filthiest old farm I had ever seen, everything you touched was dirty! I told a Land Army representative about it and that I couldn't understand how he had got his attested licence. I told him I wasn't going to work there any more and didn't. He sold up the farm soon afterwards and I think it was because he'd had his licence revoked. When my farm work finished I got a job at Woolworths in Devizes on the cosmetics counter where I worked for many years.

Dilys Fell

CHAPTER 7

Leisure time

Skating on the Crammer, *c.* 1952. The community centre, based in an old wartime U.S. Army Nissen hut, can be seen in the background.

Skating on the Canal

Skating was a great winter pastime with us. We skated on the canal and on the Crammer. Sometimes we'd skate down the canal as far as Honey Street. The favourite part of the canal, though, was the Prison Bridge pound because it was wide and there was plenty of room there but sometimes it got so crowded that to play our ice hockey games we had to set about claiming enough ice for ourselves. We would do this by congregating on the other side of the bridge and then rushing through it together in a swarm, squeezing the more genteel skaters down to the other end! We couldn't afford posh skates but I can remember buying a pair from Bowshers in the Market Place for 4/6 one night just before they closed. We were so keen to skate in those days that we took some risks, even skating as the ice was melting. If it was melted around the edges we jumped from the bank onto it and continued skating until there wasn't enough left or someone fell in! Then we packed it in.

Ralph Merrett

Swimming

We used to use the swimming pool in the canal. The water wasn't very clean and I used to get boils which I blamed on the water. There were leeches and I swear I saw a snake in the water once! I swam a lot, though, and won lots of prizes. We played polo too. Men and women swam at different times, no mixed swimming in those days! There was also a place down Foxhangers where we swam in the canal. We called it the 'skinny bath' and we used to dive off the locks into the deep water. It wasn't really safe. I used to go up to Horton at Minty's Bend and dive into the canal for Charlie Lusher, an old fisherman, and stir the mud up with my hands so that he could catch eels.

Jack Fell

Opening of the Cinema in 1912

The opening was a nine days wonder. People of the town were invited to go to the opening and it was a great occasion. We were only small children then and our grandfather took us to the second day. Performances then would usually begin with a picture flashed onto the screen of ladies dressed in their finery and saying, 'Would ladies please remove their hats'. Hats then were wide and obscured the view of people behind. I remember that the first film I saw in Devizes was *The Lady of The Lake*. I was able to boast that I had already seen this film! I had been taken to see it at The Triangle picture house in Bristol when staying there earlier with my cousins! This had been the first film I had ever seen.

Another film I saw in the same performance included a scene of a chase along a narrow street. The people who were being chased by the villains had something to do with a circus and they went up into one of the high buildings and somehow got a rope stretched across the street to the buildings opposite. They tight-roped across to escape but when the hero and heroine were

A night-time photograph taken by Ralph Merrett in about 1950 of Ivy House, a maternity hospital at the time, and the Volunteers Arms on the Green. Just to the right of the picture was a 'faggots and peas' shop run by Mrs Bond.

halfway across, the villains wrapped rags around the rope and set them on fire. Before they could reach the other side the rope burned through but by grasping hold of the rope with their hands they were able to swing to and fro, down to the street and escape!

Leonard Strong

Estcourt Statue

I was in the Market Place once, after the war, when an American lady stopped me to ask whose statue was on the fountain. I told her he was an old MP of Devizes and I said to her, 'Hey, one of your boys pinched one of these eagles from here during the War, if you see him, get him to bring it back will you'!

Jack Fell

Picnics on 'Olivers'

Another favourite place for walks was Roundway Hill and 'Olivers'. If we had friends to stay we took them there for picnics and to slide down 'Olivers' on the long grass. But, oh, the corpses! There were usually some old tree trunks lying rotting in the grass and when I was little, having heard people talking about the 'battle' on the hill, I used to think that they were the corpses! Well, I thought, they might have cleared them away, how gruesome. Years later I found that my brother had thought they were corpses too.

Lillian Hinxman

Palace Cinema

We saw all the silent films at the cinema, including the 'Sheik'

A Wadworth's staff charabanc outing, about to set off, in the 1920s.

films with Rudolph Valentino, the Buster Keaton comedies and our favourite stars such as Douglas Fairbanks, Mary Pickford and Lillian Gish. Music was provided by a piano, played while we watched. There was a children's matinee on Saturday afternoons and I used to go with John Nott and Gifford Bishop from the Elm Tree. John Nott's grandfather, George Nott, was landlord of the Volunteers Arms opposite the Green and also the town crier.

Tom Sanders

Lost in the Nettles

Each year there was a brewery trip and one year we went to Weymouth by bus. On the way back we would usually have to stop several times because the party would have drunk quite a bit on the way. We'd stop and the men went to the left and the ladies to the right, but one member of the party, by the name of Giddings fell, unnoticed,

into a bed of nettles and by the time he had climbed out again he was lost and he turned and walked back the wrong way to the bus and missed it! No-one noticed he was missing until the bus had travelled some way and although they went back for him were unable to find him for some time.

Cecil Scratchley

Entertainment in the Shop

My father was very musical and played the flute and sang. Some days there was great entertainment in the shop as people each did a turn while they waited for a haircut. Fred Tippett was a good musician, his wife had a little sweet shop next to the Prince of Wales in Sheep Street and sold toffee apples. Fred played the cornet and was in the Yeomanry. There was a chap called Chiddleton who played a one string fiddle. He used to disappear during the summer and went busking somewhere then came back in the winter, we called him 'One String Fiddler'.

Bill Underwood

Mrs Oliver's Dances

We used to go to dances at the Corn Exchange as well. I can remember Halloween Dances there with white ghosts with turnip heads and lights in them fastened to the pillars and at twelve o'clock in would come more ghosts dressed up in white shrouds! My mother would organise these events and was always planning something. She would stay in the Corn Exchange all day getting an event ready, even when she was seventy and over, she was tireless. She was known to everyone, usually, just as Mrs Oliver. She was the driving force behind lots of fetes and carnivals. We even had dances at home! We lived over my mother's shop in The Brittox, over the wool shop and over what is now the florists and was then the baby shop. The rooms are very big and we would have our meal in one of the big rooms and dance in the other one, sitting out all up the stairs.
We had a fancy dress one year and Phyllis Strong came as a cat but she lost her tail coming across The Brittox!

Peggy Hancock

Devizes Railway Station

The railway was a tremendous social centre for the town and it was a great loss when it was closed. It supported a full bookstall. My brother and I were both crazy about trains and used to

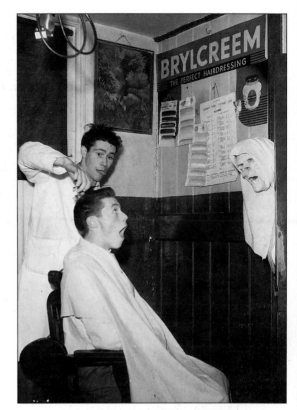

One of many 'hair raising' experiences at Underwoods in Sheep Street! Bill Underwood cuts his brother David's hair at the old shop in about 1950. Bill, and his father before him, often entertained the customers while cutting their hair.

spend hours down there. Everyone when they had visitors would go to meet them at the station and when they departed again they would go down to see them off. In the winter when people were arriving for Christmas or to stay at some other time the train might be late by an hour or so and so you would wait in the fog for it to come in. The waiting room would always have a coal fire going to keep you warm while you were waiting.

Leonard Strong

Friday night dances at the Town Hall were a popular entertainment in the 1950s. This group consists of, left to right: Bill Farmer, Mike Bowden, Sheila North, David ?, Shirley Card, Alan Scamells, Pauline Davis, Bill Underwood.

Picking Mushrooms

In September we would drive across the Plain from Urchfont towards the Bustard Inn to pick mushrooms. Sometimes the ground would be white with them. We picked them and collected them into a ladies hat box which was labelled and made ready for travelling. When it was full we closed it up and dashed back to Devizes station to catch the milk train. By first thing next morning it was at my grandmother's house in Buckhurst Hill in Essex!

Tom Sanders

London to Land's End Trials

When I was very young I used to go and help serve meals for the motorcyclists in the London to Land's End Trials. They came through Devizes in the middle of the night and stopped at White's showrooms in Sidmouth Street. It was like a big garage and the motorcyles came in one way and out the other. We served tea and coffee and buns. This must have been in the early twenties.

Peggy Hancock

Musical Entertainments

Mr Tippett was bandmaster of the town band and lived in Sheep Street and on Christmas mornings, before the war, he would ride his bike around the streets and avenues playing his trumpet to get people up and announce Christmas Day! There were lots of bands. Roundway Hospital had their own military-type band and a dance band, Mr Beavis, the head male nurse, ran these. The hospital had regular football matches and a grandstand for the patients to watch from, it was part of their entertainment, and the hospital band played at the interval.

Ice hockey on the canal near Prison Bridge, c. 1953. Ralph Merrett with home-made stick and puck (left) and Bert Maslen (right) compete before the Black Horse pub, in the background on the right.

There was a patient there at one time who had been a professional juggler and he entertained the audience at the intervals too! We used to play the staff teams at football and noticed that the patients always cheerd the visiting teams and not the staff! Some of us did musical turns on the ballroom stage at other times.

Ralph Merrett

Devizes Ladies' Choir

Mrs Butler came to Devizes and joined the Methodist Church and started a ladies choir. She had lived in India for a time and had been the conductor of the symphony orchestra in Calcutta and Principal of the School of Music. I knew her because I went to the same church and as I didn't sing I became the secretary for the choir. It was very popular for a number of years and we sang for the hospitals and old people and broadcast once for the BBC. Our best concert was probably when Mrs Butler asked the Spanish cellist Francisco Gaborra, who she had met in India, to come and play a concert with us in 1951 at the Town Hall as part of the Festival of Britain celebrations.

Violet Scudamore

Quakers Walk

This was a beautiful avenue walk in my childhood days, so carefully kept and neat, but hardly recognisable today.

Tom Sanders

Police Balls

The police balls, held in the Town Hall, before the war were wonderful

125

affairs. My husband was in the police force then and you had to be 'vetted' to go to them. Mrs Llewellyn was the Chief Constable's wife and if she didn't approve of you, you weren't allowed to go! All the police in their uniforms looked so nice but they sweated like bulls! Some of the military were invited too, the top notch, in their red coats, and I remember sitting one night at the town hall, and seeing Colonel Guy. He had a stiff shirt on with his red coat, and as I looked along the row I saw that his shirt had bowed out at the front, they were only tucked in at the sides, and you could see straight through it and out the other side! I never forgot that. The band from the Pump Room at Bath played there sometimes and the pianist sang light classical songs to dance to. They were really exciting, something to look back on.

Peggy Hancock

Cinema Fires

The Palace has twice been burned down. The second time was in 1932 which was when I was about to return from London to work in my father's business. While the cinema was being rebuilt I can remember we went to the Corn Exchange to see films.

Leonard Strong

Allotments

We had an allotment down Pans Lane and another one at London Road where the police headquarters is.

We had all kinds of soft fruits at Pans Lane: strawberries, raspberries, loganberries, gooseberries, red, white and black-currants. We'd go down there in the summer and after we had picked them my mother made pots and pots of jam and jelly.

Gwen Chivers

Singing Lessons

The room at the back in Handel House, behind the shop, was used as a music room, and a teacher came up from Bath, Valerie Christopher, who had pupils for singing lessons on Thursdays. I had some lessons from her myself when I took part in *HMS Pinafore* with the operatic society. I was Little Buttercup when I was ten years old.

Peggy Hancock

Bertie Bushnell

Bertie Bushnell was a drover and vagrant who used to sleep up at Gipsy Patch in a tent. If he got ill he would go up to St James' Hospital, which was the workhouse, and they'd give him a bath and a bed and when he got better he'd go back to his tent. He was a real character, everyone knew Bertie Bushnell!

Gwen Chivers